The Lighthouse Keeper

Essays on the Poetry of

Eleanor Ross Taylor

ભ   ભ   ભ

Jean Valentine, Editor

Hobart and William Smith Colleges Press
Geneva, New York

Special thanks to an anonymous donor who made the publication of this book possible. Thanks as well to Elaine Sinniger, Susan Reece, Pat Blakeslee, and Peg Kowalik for their invaluable support.

Grateful acknowledgment is made to the following publishers for permission to reprint work in this volume: Poems from *Late Leisure* reprinted by permission of Louisiana State University Press, © 1999 by Eleanor Ross Taylor. Poems from *Days Going / Days Coming Back* reprinted by permission of University of Utah Press, © 1991 by University of Utah Press. Poems reprinted in *Days Going / Days Coming Back* were originally published in: *Wilderness of Ladies*, McDowell, Obolensky, 1960; *Welcome Eumenides*, George Braziller, 1972; and *New and Selected Poems*, Stuart Wright, 1983. Lorrie Goldensohn's "The Gardener of Ghosts" was part of a review first published in *Parnassus: Poetry in Review*, Vol. 18, No. 2 / Vol. 19, No. 1, 1993. Richard Howard's Foreword to *Welcome Eumenides* was published in that volume by George Braziller, 1972. Randall Jarrell's Introduction to *Wilderness of Ladies* was published in that volume by McDowell, Obolensky, 1960. Adrienne Rich's "Woman Observing, Preserving, Conspiring, Surviving: The Poems of Eleanor Ross Taylor" was published in *The New York Times Book Review*, July 2, 1972, and in *On Lies, Secrets, and Silence*, W.W. Norton, 1979, reprinted by permission of the author. Henry Taylor's "Woman Singing: The Poems of Eleanor Ross Taylor" was first published in *Sewanee Review*, Winter 2001. Ellen Bryant Voigt's essay is excerpted from "Structural Subversion," published in *The Flexible Lyric*, reprinted by permission of University of Georgia Press, © 2000 by Ellen Bryant Voigt. Alan Williamson's "Between Two Worlds: The Poetry of Eleanor Ross Taylor" is excerpted from *Eloquence and Mere Life*, and reprinted by permission of University of Michigan Press, © 1994 by Alan Williamson.

Cover: Photograph of Eleanor Ross Taylor by Miriam Berkley; design by Peg Kowalik. Printed on recycled paper by Syracuse Litho.

ISBN 0-934888-17-5
Hobart and William Smith Colleges Press
Demarest Hall
Hobart and William Smith Colleges
Geneva, New York 14456

CONTENTS

Introduction

To our knowledge and memory there have not yet been many women poets of genius: Eleanor Ross Taylor is one. She moves oddly and freely from narratives to sustained dramatic monologues to brief lyrics, at home in them all. Her work is quirky, intelligent, passionate and profound. She is a brilliant elegist who has written laments for historical figures, for her parents, for her mentor and friend Randall Jarrell, and for the unlived life (which turns out, in the paradox of poetry, to be the life she is living).

Eleanor Taylor says that when she was in her twenties and thirties, Jarrell would say to her, "Are you writing?" And she'd say no, and he'd say, "You'll be sorry. God will make you sorry." And of course he was right. Here is a poem from the late '80s, "At the Altar":

> That bag you packed me
> when you sent me
> to the universe —
> camp after camp I've opened it
> debating whether to unpack —
>   *Not yet, not yet* —
> Why did I feel so much in it
> was dangerous on the playground,
> too good for everyday,
> feel those splendid fireworks
> hazardous to institutions,
> unmannerly to etiquette,
> so that, time after time,
> I found myself saying
>   *Not yet?*
>
> At each new place I faced it,
> it suggested,
> Here spread out your things,
> put on this coat,
> open this bottle —
>   *No, not yet . . .*

sometimes throwing something out,
giving things away,
lightening my load. . . .

The more I pull out,
the more it seems, some days,
is left inside,
the heavier it is.

Sometimes I think this package
is almost a door
the opening of which
careening across heaven
could be fatal.

Some days now I wonder if I'll ever
dare face my given garments —
permanently wrinkled,
surely out of date —
your travel-thought
wasting in its tissue, flesh-corrupt —
till I've absorbed it,
like those stitches that dissolve
in an incision
where something's been removed.

Taylor's conflict and pain speak clearly enough for this woman's dilemma: to be or not to be a poet, to follow or not her *wyrd*, her destiny. For most of Taylor's life, her love for poetry — for *writing* poetry (God's "travel-thought") — was in a standoff with her allegiance to family, to the southern family woman that she was and is; she says she didn't *work* at her poetry until she was almost seventy. Tradition is no abstraction; it is flesh and blood.

On the other hand, look at what she did before she *worked*! Her dilemma became her destiny.

Much of Taylor's poetry, musical as it is, *worked* as it is, comes to us in fragments, almost notes.

. . . the trail breaks off,
scent's lost. Wandering is
the only way out of this place.
— "The Diary"

There have always been brilliant voices to praise Eleanor Ross Taylor: one of the first, and most famous, that of Randall Jarrell. I started to think about this *festschrift* with that first core of already published pieces in mind: Jarrell, Richard Howard, Adrienne Rich, Lorrie Goldensohn, Alan Williamson, and Ellen Bryant Voigt. Robert Lowell and Elizabeth Bishop loved her work, but never wrote about it, and many other poets as well; I set about to ask some of the living.

And, like friendship, one person led to another.

Randall Jarrell wrote the introduction to Taylor's first book, *A Wilderness of Ladies* (1960); when he received the National Book Award he said that he wished she had won it, so that her poems would find more readers; he placed her with Dickinson, Moore, and Bishop in our western sky.

Richard Howard likewise praised and introduced her next book, *Welcome Eumenides* (1972), placing her again next to Dickinson, and to Whitman. Adrienne Rich also praised that book in *The New York Times Book Review*, and more recently, in a blurb for *Late Leisure* (1999) calls Taylor "one of the 'lighthouse keepers' of the century."

Lorrie Goldensohn and Alan Williamson both wrote searching, thoughtful essays in response to her lifework that far, on the occasion of the publication of *Days Going / Days Coming Back* (1991); this was especially fitting because in her *New and Selected Poems* (1984) and in *Days Going* Taylor chose to reprint some of the poems from her earlier books as well: a way of keeping her strongest work in print from one decade to the next.

In her essay "Structural Subversion," Ellen Bryant Voigt explored Taylor's subversion of the southern narrative structure: "the grit provoking the pearl."

Of our new writers, I am lucky to have found a variety of willing souls: women and men, younger and older, some who know Taylor, most who don't; some Southern, some Northern, some Other. In thinking about the order the essays should take I tried first alphabetical, for its democratic simplicity, and was happy with its serendipities.

Betty Adcock's essay helps us, as Heather Ross Miller's does, to imagine intimately the South this woman poet came out of.

Fred Chappell, like Henry Taylor, writes about the poet's life-work this far: both have done scrupulous, far-reaching critical essays. Ben Cleary gives us a glimpse of "the writer at work" in his loving account of a visit with the Taylors to a country church where the poet saw the altar needlework that she later made into a country-church-and-universe poem.

Alfredo Franco has chosen A Wilderness of Ladies to concentrate his meditations on. Thoughtfully he notes how one poem plays off against another, one image against another, in this house, and wilderness—of voices. Eric Gudas begins with Late Leisure and works back, finding her lifework formidable, idiosyncratic, passionate. Jim Harms talks about silence and the nature of time in her work, moving from her study of the workings of consciousness to her feminist poetics, her linguistic complications. Greg Orr has given us a still, winter prose poem that embodies the act of reading this poetry, its "fierce slants and zig-zags."

Deborah Tall has written about Taylor's risk-taking, her density, her compression, her thirst; and in the end has thanked her, as we all must, for being a good guide. And Rosanna Warren has lit up Taylor's rhythms, her parts of speech, her poems "hip to the world's sorrow as to its plenitude and oddness."

It has been an honor and a joy to read each of these pieces as they have come in. Each one has taught me better how to read this beloved poet; all of them together, like her poems themselves, make up much more than the sum of their parts, make up a bright first book of homage to this classic living among us.

ભ   ભ   ભ

I want to thank Dave Smith for his generous encouragement and help, right from the start. I have untellable gratitude for the authors of this book, for their ardent work. Deborah Tall and the Hobart and William Smith Colleges Press have given the book its "travel-thought."

And most of all, we all thank Eleanor Ross Taylor herself, for being our source.

Betty Adcock

The Piano in the Kitchen

In my deep-south rural childhood, a certain poor family lived on a played-out farm far out in the country. This family, like my better-off one, like everybody's, had lived in that county for many generations, all our ancestors having come to East Texas from North Carolina, Virginia, or Middle Tennessee; and having brought with them a plantation economy with all its attendant ills. Thus settled in that unusually lush strip of earliest Texas, they lived out the bitter, bloody history of the south.

This particular poor family's run-down kitchen held a magnificent but utterly ruined rosewood piano which had been put to use as an extra table and kitchen work surface. Brought—at what cost?—to a wilderness a hundred years before, it was both present and lost. Stories like this are common in the south; in one place it might be a set of ragged law books, in another a grime-caked painting or a mysteriously valuable piece of jewelry—something from a gone other life, now ignored or put to odd use. I can imagine this piano, this dense contradiction, in an Eleanor Ross Taylor poem. She has drawn many of her dream-like lyrics from the world which held such ornate and battered silences:

> Her house was screenless; doors stood wide;
> Leaves drifted unwatched down the hall;
> Hens left warm eggs indoors.
> . . . . .
> For she was always in the low-grounds
> Chopping cotton, or by the orchard
> Binding wheat with wheat-strands,
> Thinning the corn slips in the new-ground field,
> Then home to snatch the coffee pot
> Up off the floor (where the baby'd played),
> Lay table, before they all got in.
>
> —Kate, this brew's not fit to drink.
> —What? . . .
> > > > Oh Lord.
> . . . . .

I never cried for shirtwaists
Or China cups
Or crocheted pillow shams. I've not.
But oh to have it said of me
She boiled the gosling in the coffee pot. . . .

—"Epitaph"

Taylor's poems create a highly individual but completely recognizable experience of woman *in* the south, *of* the south, and of a certain time, born into a certain class, inheriting—along with the silver spoons—a set of constrictions, duties, desires, and guilts unknown to men (who had other demons). Often the double message of fallen grandeur and the necessity for hardscrabble work existed in the same extended family. In "Completing the Pilgrimage," the speaker acknowledges her kinship with "all . . . in this backwoods . . . /The idiot brother. The crazy uncle, too./The white-browed figure/in a black plush/hat off some Colonial shelf. . . . "

I am younger than Eleanor Ross Taylor by some twenty years, but the rural south did not change much in the time between her childhood and mine. I too remember eccentric elegance, faded grace, wild transgressing, ghosts, serious guilts, and the beauty of the ruined, burgeoning, threatening land that shines though her poems. I remember too the stranglehold of that intense presence in Taylor's work: the straitjacket of expectations in which southern white women were destined to live. Randall Jarrell, in his wise introduction to Taylor's first book, called ours the Puritan south, that Scots-Irish Presbyterianism outlasting defeat, comeuppance, and modernization:

You dish potatoes up three times a day
And put your wedding dress into a quilt.
. . . . .
. . . a sisterhood in multiple rosettes,
Adoring our Victorian regrets.

—"The Bine Yadkin Rose"

Taylor was writing the poem, from which those lines were taken, in the 1950s. There simply were no southern women poets with a body of work at that time, and no feminism as we know it. She was writing something entirely new—the lives of southern white women. "Playing," a poem utilizing folk speech, children's games, southern landscape, and what women could expect, is an example of some of Taylor's most interesting qualities. This is the whole poem:

In Ugly Creek they dashed their toes.
The Cyril Mabry cows arose
And water spiders stepped aside
To watch how little girls would wade;
A summer picnic well delayed
Might miss the churn-turned fireside.

Those old folks always have been old . . .
Those childhoods tell-re-over-told
Are just a pocket full of seeds
That never generated weeds. . . .

When the little girls returned to the bank
Their little fingers swelled and shrank!
A frigid, leafless shadow lay
Upon the water-throated day.
They piled their hands to play a game—
Pretense had always been their aim. . . .
What was it, little girls became?
Take if off, knock it off, or
Have the crows peck it off—?
The little hands . . . they somehow shake;
The little bones they somehow quake.

Where's my share? Cat got it.
Where's cat? In the woods.
Where's woods? Water squenched.
Where's ox? Rope lynched.
Where's rope? "Dead and buried
Behind the new church door
And the first that laughs or grins or shows
His teeth
Gets a slap, and a kick, and a knock, and a—
Wreath."

The female bitter black tongues hum
The palms forsake the stiffened thumb
(The waiting womb! the waiting tomb —
The empty antique sitting room!)
Before the final griefs succumb —

ROBERT, YOU LEFT OUT SOME!
You left out some!
You left out some!
Watt . . . left out some . . .

This children's game in a creek is macabre, as children's games often are. And it may be deadly indeed. The question "What was it, little girls became?" following the statement "Pretense had always been their aim" certainly goes deeper than games. The penultimate stanza is spoken in the adult voice of prophecy remembered. "Playing" shocks us with its acid wit, its fierce pantomime of children, its *knowing*. The already cruel litany that accompanies little hands piling on hands becomes more serious, more true, in the sing-song patterned next-to-last stanza. In the last stanza, the child's voice returns to accuse the makers of games, the makers too of the hard contingencies waiting for little girls. The adult speaker's sudden return to the child's voice here is chilling and seems to present the child discovering ahead, as the adult has looked back to see, that the harshest possibilities were "left out."

ଓ ଓ ଓ

With a potent blend of elegance and colloquialism, Taylor created poems powerful enough to contain the sheer longing of women corseted by a culture that bade them be nice, be neat, be nurturing. The poems also embody contradiction, the clear tension between the speaker's wish to fly free and the wish to keep to her ordained role. In the "The Chain Gang Guard," a poem from her first book, the guard is as much a captive as those he watches. The prisoners are free to taunt passersby, to flirt with pretty women going past, while the guard must be silent lest the women (and/or the prisoners) make fun of him. The prisoners here are wild instinct, unbridled sexuality, a kind of freedom in their very being. The guard is himself the most imprisoned, and by his own choosing. In the last stanza he says:

> If I had ever learned to tear-up-jack,
> Got drunk enough to leave myself behind,
> Could know which time to take and which to pay—
> Here I stand! loaded gun across me—
> As if I'd get away!

And in the poem "Cousin Ida" the speaker states point-blank:

> I, captive, cage-fond,
> Dread doors opening on the great beyond.
> That bird they said had no song of her own
> Cries from the black gum to my ears alone. . . .

ଓଃ   ଓଃ   ଓଃ

Taylor has said in an essay that she had no tradition. I will go so far as to use a trendy term I dislike and say that she had to invent herself. The term "original" appears in nearly all reviews or comments on her work. We hear much about women creating a new language to say what they alone have known. Taylor managed it *within* modernism, and within the south—an outsider all the same—among a gaggle of New Critics. She spoke lives that had been mute as ravaged piano strings in a backwoods kitchen.

> They bound me up in ribbons, moiré bows,
> My hair so tight it left no play for face,
> My waist so tight it left no space for plea.
> "Child, you'll be miserable," they warned, "Don't go,"
> (Stay here where suffering's homemade, sure to fit.)
> Mine never has worn out, though it's grown thin
> Now, like a veil. I see through it
> When the shadows are right. Light dwindles
> In the outer world, and my own ember,
> Knocked about like a goody in a nut,
> Shines smally through—dormant—convoluted—
> Half a notion to spill out.
>
> —"Cousin Ida"

The intertwined, braided music of the second and third lines enacts the tight-laced life to which the girl is condemned. Line five in this excerpt extends the clothing metaphor from the admonition to stay here where the suffering's homemade and sure to fit. The cloth, the dress, the covering made of that suffering "never has worn out" but has grown thin, like a veil (bridal or mourning veil, or both?) and the speaker sees through it "when the shadows are right." Sees through, as to see the reality behind it? Or sees through, as to have one's vision altered (or enhanced?) by looking at the world through this time-thinned veil, these memories.

Earlier in the poem Cousin Ida tells us:

> One year I clapped my hand over my eyes
> When spring came, and when I took it down
> My knuckles were speckled brown.
> In the middles, in the red cotton bloom,
> Each warm clod with its darker side,
> Its sprouting seeds of the staved-off jungle,
> Slaves still sang . . .

It was when spring came that the girl clapped her hand over her eyes, as if to prevent herself from seeing the burgeoning, the sexual, the coming to flower of world or self. When she took the hand down, she was old . . . having missed, what? Everything? "In the middles," she tells us, "slaves still sang." This "in the middles" being the time her eyes were covered. How much she did not see is subtly underlined.

ଔ   ଔ   ଔ

Late Leisure, the collection published in 1999 when Taylor was 79, shows her sidelong lyricism undiminished. One poem from that book, "Shaking the Plum Tree," shows again her instinct for mystery at the center of a keenly observed world:

> Such light there was.
> Ben up the plum tree,
>   red plums snaked with light,
> gold veins jagging in the plum skins

> like metal boiling,
> plums bolting, knocking, to the ground,
>   the sky, a huge shade-tree of light
> tenting the stubblefield with centigrade,
>   the pine woods' lashes, glass,
>   the girls' frocks, pale with glare,
>   the voile geraniums, fading,
> only the sheer hats shading
>   the jelly cheeks dark red
> and the simmering eyes,
>   coming to a boil.

Typical of Taylor's work is the perfect accuracy of "plums snaked with light,/gold veins jagging in the plum skins," and that sky "tenting the stubblefield with centigrade." As for the metaphor running the length of the one long sentence from line two until the end, jelly-making that is really the sexual simmer in summer air like glass, it is original and funny, and frightening as well. "Ben" comes right after the opening light, a boy up a plum tree shaking down the bounty. His position is dominant, but he is not the engineer of these doings.

Taylor's use of the language of the country south of an earlier time, a mixture of the earthy, the ungrammatical, and the elegant, shows her to have near-perfect pitch. "Stretched me aright smart," says the old woman who has crossed the river of her dying as the boat slips back a little so that she must stretch to reach the other shore. The crickets who cry toward the future are saying, "Fall is yonder." The speaker in one poem says, "I looked for/you a cattail but/they were all silked out." In "Song," the speaker says, "I have the clipping tells all about it,/If your Grandma aint thrown it out." And from the wonderful poem "Family Bible," the following history:

> My full name is Aminta Dunlap Watkins Ross.
> My mother was Merina Wilkerson.
> My father was Arnold Watkins—he carpentered—
> I married your pa Whitson Ross
> My wedding presents were a feather bed and two hens.

ଔ   ଔ   ଔ

A well-brought-up North Carolina girl from the country, Taylor as a young woman would have been as familiar with poor dirt farmers as with the gently shabby, the eccentric, and the patrician. An isolated backwater could offer remarkable diversity (of a certain kind) in those days. The Woman's College of the University of North Carolina at Greensboro gave her a solid education—nicely separated from males, of course. She married Peter Taylor, a son of old Memphis society and one of the group of writers loosely connected to the Fugitives, that core of poets and New Critics who came to dominate American poetry. Peter Taylor became one of the south's most respected fiction writers. Their circle of friends included many of the most important poets in America, John Crowe Ransom, Allen Tate, Robert Penn Warren, Randall Jarrell, Robert Lowell, and—as the shy poet might say—*then some!* What was it like for her among those distinguished, competitive, brilliant men who were utterly sure of their places in the firmament of poetry? Other wives in that circle wrote, but they wrote prose. I've heard it said that admirers of Peter Taylor at the University of Virginia, where he taught, would sometimes add, "I hear his wife writes too." What must it have been like for her, with her peculiar gifts, her unforgiving intelligence, her sensitivity, shyness, and puritan conscience?

Randall Jarrell was no doubt instrumental in getting her first book of poems published. Perhaps her work would not have seen the light of day without the support of such readers. And Jarrell wrote an admiring introduction to her first book in 1960. Somewhere in that introduction, he names her "(as the census would say) housewife." The demurral does not quite cover what might be construed as condescension in his strong praise. Later, he says that the poems' originality is "so entire, yet so entirely natural, that it seems something their writer deserves no credit for: she could do no other." High praise, yes, but with something in it that implies that she didn't know what she was doing. Jarrell admired Taylor's work enormously, and perhaps we can hold the times responsible for the sexist observation, but it remains troubling. It is a clue, I think, to what it must have been like in the center of that vortex of literary activity, where Eleanor was perhaps passing canapés and was certainly raising children.

Though her isolation was totally different from Emily Dickinson's, it may not have been less intense.

ભ   ભ   ભ

Two kinds of struggle vie for dominance in Taylor's poems. There is the struggle with the bleak and universal harshness of just living, of time and loss, of love even, of death certainly, and of unfulfilled hope. Then there is the internal struggle, the self against the self, internalized war willed to her by ancestors, church, culture. Here are the battles of flesh and duty, of joy and anguish, of wish against necessity.

Many poems show a delight in family, amusement at foibles, love indeed—but along with these, there is a repugnance shading toward terror, as of entrapment, and the guilt such emotions engage. Yet poem after poem shows that the imprisonment of the women who speak is at least partly of their own choosing. To quote a phrase from one poem and the title of another, Taylor is both "cage-fond" and "contemplating jailbreak." In a poem in which the poet is clearly herself the speaker, she says, "I'm constructing my own brierpatch." Br'er Rabbit of southern folktale was shrewd indeed. Perhaps Taylor, with her *given* conflicts, has constructed precisely the right space for herself.

In these lyrics, female *dailiness*—duty and hatred of duty, the games of memory, the snares of marriage, the drag of the family net—becomes true drama. In the poet's hands, authentic inner life and outer world are never ordinary, are shapeshifting in rhythm with emotions as radical and conflicted and powerful as any in literature. Writing at a time when academic professionalism was becoming prerequisite for poets, Taylor had to have felt herself alone in the midst of consummate professionals. And she was writing in voices that had not been heard before, had not been thought important enough to be written into poems. The fire for her forge was the very life, with its restrictions and conflicts, its history and requirements, that would have seemed hellbent on keeping her from writing. That flame could flare, suddenly unruly and dangerous, into a poem like "Woman as

Artist," in which the following excerpts leap strangely out of the
year 1960, the year of its publication:

> I'm mother.
> I hunt alone.
> There is no bone
> Too dry for me, mother,
> Or too extra.
> . . . . .
> An emigrant from the mother tongue
> To say-so in the silent one,
> For me the stepped-for step sinks,
> The expected light winks
> Out; dear self, do not think
> On the ominous appetite rising insistently
> In the hour of no food. . . .
> . . . . .
> Kneel, fathers.
> If my babies are right,
> It is not because of you!
> . . . . .
> Next year I'll dig them up
> And separate them.
> They'll multiply
>   Multiply
>   Multiply
> Till the round earth's ringed with Babel trumpets,
> Some dark, some light,
> Some streakèdy.

In such a poem we see a fierce intelligence awake and angry, despairing but carrying a dark humor . . . managing the latter in
phrases that carry the mother-wit of folk speech in "no
bone/Too dry . . ./Or too extra"; and the wonderful metamor-
phosis of "babies" (standing as poems, creations of the woman
as artist) into flower bulbs, ready to ring the world with "Babel
trumpets," with blossoms of language . . . "Some dark, some
light/Some streakèdy."

Again and again her poems contain such phrases, part of the
earthy, provincial speech she'd have heard growing up, phrases
that ought to strike the reader's ear as awkward, but turn out to
be exactly, oddly, perfectly right.

She constructs also a diction of sophisticated disassociation:

> The cars that pass us eye us curiously —
> Stodged with our eyes, our frozen triggers cocked
>
> — "The Chain Gang Guard"

> . . . . shells of water momentary,
> guile of colored light,
> gray moonstone tears
> of loss and irrecovery.
>
> — "The Bubble"

> I would have disfestooned my world —
> A husband, more or less!
> A family, more or less! —
>
> — "Sister"

And this marvelous description of a ghost:

> From the moment Gabriella died
> At an exhausted, nightless morning time
> A knifestruck disattendance cast a gloom. . . .
>
> — "Wind"

The humor in Taylor's poems is a surprise, sometimes dark, sometimes just wonderful fun. In a clever play on the obsessions of southerners with their lines of descent, she writes:

> Let those in ascendancy
> Have dominion
> Over those in descendancy.
> Ascend, descendants.
> . . . . .
> Bury the ladder and scend no more.

Whether for mirth, for beauty, or for bitter truth, she finds or invents the words she needs, put to uses we'd not have imagined, notes from a "stanched" music.

ભ   ભ   ભ

Not so finely tuned as Elizabeth Bishop, yet like her in precision of description; and not so coldly armored as Marianne
Moore; not confessional, not overtly feminist, not experimental
in any way that could have earned her entry into any of succes-
sive avant-gardes, and something of a recluse, Eleanor Ross Taylor may never receive the wide recognition she deserves. She is
perhaps too eccentric, too much the outsider, too distant from
the engines of literary promotion. She is rooted in an unfashionable region, and her work is difficult. Some poems can seem to
be puzzles whose pieces are too scattered for the picture to make
itself known to us. A poet friend once said to me, "I don't think
she *wants* people to understand those poems." And it is true that
the art of concealment is very much a part of this work. But as
any poet knows, this is part of the dance, and the code is not
meant to exclude us entirely. The poems are like half-wild things
that elude us as a glimpsed bird might do, or one who cries
"Lost!" but does not really wish or expect to be found. And yet
she has laid a trail into the wilderness:

Find Me

by my trail of fragments,
                                        stale crumbs,
        green broken boughs
        of protocol.

Those who follow this path will find the "staved-off jungle," the
backwoods that lived behind all the small towns and neat farms
of the south; and they will find that wilderness of protocol in
which white women, unfed in so many ways and nearly unseen,
lived their lives. Readers will find also the "Wilderness of Ladies," which lasted decades past the Victorian age in this region,
signifying educated women consigned to ignorance, sharp intelligence consigned to gossip, cornbread, quilts. It may also signify
the wilderness *in* those ladies, whose lively hearts and bodies
might well go native, given half a chance. It is interesting to note

that Taylor has written several poems from the point of view of women captured by Indians. That these various shades of meaning persist in Taylor's use of the term "wilderness" is exactly the point. She is a master of unlikely kinships.

Her voices can surprise us mightily. Usually drawn from her native region, they also range as far as Florence Nightingale's diaries and imagined thoughts in the brilliant eight-page poem "Welcome Eumenides." And in a long poem titled "A Few Days in the South in February," Taylor speaks as Mister S. K. Wightman, father of a Union soldier, who has come to North Carolina ("into the land of the enemy") in 1865 to retrieve his son's body at all costs. Richard Howard has called this the best poem about the Civil War since Whitman.

I place Taylor in the company of two other fierce and reticent souls: Emily Dickinson, whom she resembles in creating a nearly private music; and Elizabeth Bishop, who knows the story's in the details and whose strict lyricism operates in the service of an observed world. Bishop's sense of privacy and loss are, like Taylor's, part of the fabric of her poems. Gregory Orr has said in an essay that Bishop may outlast Lowell. I believe that if readers and critics follow Taylor's trail of crumbs to her particular wilderness, she will be seen to be a stronger poet than some of the celebrated dinner guests at Peter Taylor's table.

It is worth noting that Taylor was forty when she published her first book in 1960, that it was twelve years before she published a second, eleven years between the second and the third. Her books have often been short, and many contain selections from earlier books as well as new poems, so her overall output has been small. Here are the first and last stanzas of "At the Altar":

> That bag you packed me
> when you sent me
> to the universe—
> camp after camp I've opened it
> debating whether to unpack—
>   *Not yet, not yet*—
> Why did I feel so much in it
> was dangerous on the playground,
> too good for everyday,

feel those splendid fireworks
hazardous to institutions,
unmannerly to etiquette,
so that, time after time,
I found myself saying
    Not yet?
. . . . .
Some days now I wonder if I'll ever
dare face my given garments—
permanently wrinkled,
surely out of date—
your travel-thought
wasting in its tissue, flesh-corrupt—
till I've absorbed it,
like those stitches that dissolve
in an incision
where something's been removed.

The speaker seems to be addressing God, in sorrow that there were some gifts she never opened, some things she was afraid to try; that perhaps she did not live up to her potential as an artist or realize her potential for happiness. The last line chills into perfect loss, lost time, lost opportunity. Here is a veiled yet clear instance of the poet's owning up to fears, reluctances, and complicity in her own imprisonment.

Another poem published in the same book creates a kind of parallel. Titled simply "No," it is the account of a woman on a bus. The speaker is observing this woman who behaves erratically, rummages continually in an overstuffed plastic bag or shakes her head ("a run of negatives . . . ") compulsively. The piece has both the dense observation and the cool detachment of a poem by Bishop. Its details reveal the speaker as well as the crazy woman. The woman rummaging in the bag slides out a worn, stag-handled knife with a longish blade and lays it beside her on an empty seat, where it simply stays when the woman moves to another part of the bus. The knife rides on the seat across from the speaker "in independent menace." Eventually the woman notices and retrieves the knife and holds it on her lap. Resuming the compulsive head-shaking, she takes up her routine:

becomes again the metronome
that drums no tune—
no
no
no

It's impossible not to see a strange parallel between the woman afraid of her gifts in "At the Altar" and her mirror opposite, the woman rummaging in her bag on the bus. "*Not Yet! Not Yet!*" says the privileged one; "*no no no*" says the mad one. One owns a bag not unpacked out of fear and propriety; one unpacks her sad history in public, and draws from her bulging trashbag a knife, something certainly "hazardous to institutions" and "unmannerly to etiquette." Like the chain-gang prisoners who can sing and holler at passing people, the madwoman is a kind of freedom. *And it is awful.* Eleanor Ross Taylor cuts herself no slack.

Poetry like this is tied in so many knots it is very like life itself, very like the inner world we know, even if we are not southerners. If, as W.H. Auden once said, "Poetry is the clear expression of mixed feelings," then Eleanor Ross Taylor writes the truest poetry I have found.

ભ   ભ   ભ

That image of a scarred rosewood piano stays with me. Piled with fruit jars, lard buckets, dinner leftovers, it wears in my fancy a patina of cornbread crumbs, a sweet stain of fig preserves. There's a serious mystery in its story, a ghost, as if a Bach fugue haunted the biscuits, hovered around the syrup pitcher, hummed in the clabber pan. No one knew any longer what journey that piano had taken, or whose hands had last touched its keys for melody and love. Yet it was *there*, big as a rhinoceros and just as incongruous, testament and proof, riddle and chastisement. In its doubleness, its contradictory existence, it is kin to the mysteries in Taylor's poems. In my imagination, she sits down at that lost instrument, lard buckets and all, and begins to play.

Fred Chappell

The "Voltaged" Language of Eleanor Ross Taylor

Critics, reviewers, and readers are unanimous. Eleanor Ross Taylor's poetry is unique. Adjectives such as "startling," "individual," "quirky," "odd," "original," "daring and innovative," and "unexpected" are strewn through descriptions of her work. She is rarely compared to other poets, but when she is, the names of Emily Dickinson and Marianne Moore are mentioned, though not in terms of probable influence. These comparisons seem to be agile but misplaced attempts to find some bases of judgment. A more apt comparison might be with the poems of her niece, Heather Ross Miller, but these poems are less well known than they should be.

Granted, that terms like "unique" and "individual" and even "quirky" are common critical coin nowadays; poets feel obliged to establish personal voices and even mannerisms. In earlier periods—during the eighteenth century, say—they were supposed to avoid oddness and to exhibit their strengths by working skillfully within an established tradition. There are feasible reasons why we can regard Dr. Johnson's heroic couplets as being superior to Joseph Addison's; there are comprehensible reasons for saying that Pope "improved" upon Dryden. But in contemporary poetry, where strong individualism is the rule, it requires an extraordinary style to stand out from the mass.

If Taylor does so—and I agree with the majority opinion in this case—it might be useful to try to see why hers is so different from other work, what makes it so particular in its excellences. The large matters of her highly personal vision and strain of thought will be paramount in any extended discussion, as will her choice of materials, autobiographical and historical. The tradition to which her work belongs will perhaps be germane; Allen Tate classified her as "a formalist in a mode that must be described as epigrammatic lyricism," and his observation seems just in outline, though much too limited.

A narrower examination—as mine must be at this time—will have to focus upon her techniques and there is a handsome array of these to look at, strategies that help to make a Taylor poem display the unmistakable hand of Eleanor. Her rhythms—spiky, abrupt, staccato—are characteristic, as is her use of dialogue, of which she gives only sharp snippets for the most part, trusting a swift phrase, an idiosyncratic word to produce rapid impressions of her speakers. There is the look of her pages, in which short lines end or start with breathless dashes, trail off into regretful or introspective ellipses, or clench up at the end with question marks. I sometimes feel I can already hear the sound of a Taylor poem without reading a word; its appearance on the page suggests, once it is known, her sensibility.

But for me it is her diction which gives her work its peculiar and bittersweet tang. Her language is like no one else's. When Donald Hall coined the term "McPoem" to describe the nondescript product of so many contemporaries, he found the perfect antonym for a Taylor poem.

My bare avowals are, of course, more than a little weak as critical analysis, and so I offer here some preliminary observations of certain aspects of the poet's diction. None of them separately, and not all of them together, are sufficient to add up to what we will recognize as her characteristic style, yet these techniques aid in the formative process and they are more feasibly open to brief review than are the larger concerns of vision and perspective.

The following elements are salient: Taylor's strange adjectives and adverbs; some of her nouns and nonce words, especially her compounds; her sudden excursions into colloquial or "country" diction in formal contexts; her puns; her infrequent but outlandish personifications; her coinages; and most especially, most particularly to be remarked, her verbs.

Modifiers are probably the easiest terms with which poets find originality. The sense of a sentence is only adorned or more finely tuned by an adjective or adverb and, though the search for the just one may be long, a poem does not often live or die by these parts of speech. In her choice of modifiers, Eleanor Ross

Taylor is as daring as in her other usages — but not continually so. Any other strong poet might refer to the sound of a falling tree as a "*dirging* crash" ("Overgrown Path") or refer to a bishop's "*balconied* Te Deum" ("A Place Apart"), or even describe goblets as being "*sotted* with dust" ("Dust"). [My emphases.] These words are unusual but they are hardly wayward; they don't fiercely call attention to themselves, more concerned with underlining images than with illuminating them.

But when we find a cat described as "washing *stand-by* feet in idle ablution" ("Gainesville, March"; my emphasis) we feel at once the shiver at recognizing an unusual mind, a freshened eye. It is a true adjective, just and witty, but it is utterly original and could issue only from Taylor's sensibility and from no other's. When some readers compare her language to Marianne Moore's, I believe they must be remembering her infrequent use of rare adjectives like "globose," used to describe newborn babies ("Maternity Ward"), or "pilose," which describes newborn mice ("Trouble"). Taylor does not find her words with a jeweler's loupe, as Moore seems to do; her rarities are not set in her poems like gems in platinum bracelets. They are there because they are necessary.

If modifiers are the less original parts of Taylor's vocabulary, still there are some that sparkle with her temperament, terms that no one else ever would have employed. Taylor alone would use "trompe l'oeil" as an adverb to describe a fledgling dove "sliding" among flowers ("August Doves") or refer to deer seen occasionally during a car ride as "intersticial" ("Va. Sun. A. M. Dec. '73") or describe a flower garden as "histrionic" ("Buck Duke and Mamma"). Who else would use "jinni" as an adverb? "Or some wretch in my family past/. . . come navigate/my sleep,/and wring his trauma out?/rise jinni in my blood?/say that he's me?" ("Hatchways")

She has a fondness for compound modifiers, partly because of her relentless urge toward compression. With compounds she can load a lot of meaning into a single set of terms, multiplying the ironies by which her poetry thrives. In "The Bine Yadkin Rose," she calls the life of a woman who has taken a temporary position as a seamstress "a scissorly-wise drama"; in "Playing,"

a pond that reflects the sky is seen as "the water-throated day";
the light that illumines the baseboards in a dusty old house in
"Night" is "spider-bagged"; a long Tennessee valley is "breath-
stealing" in "Katydids Sewanee." In the little allegorical exercise,
"Kitchen Fable," the fork is able to handle "nonforthcoming
pickles,/defiant stretched-out lettuce,/sauce-gooed particles."
Leaves in late summer trees are "first-loosening" ("August
Doves") and the cracked streets of Gambier, Ohio, are "time-
quaked." The first stanza of "One Last Warm Day" exhibits a
display case of her silvery modifier usages:

> One last warm day
> on the devised chair
> on the devised floor,
> aura of tree,
> its canned sun spewing
> mixed-spectrum stars.

Here the density of imagery and language is so intense that
one might recall Gerard Manley Hopkins and his extremely precise observations of nature taut in the Gordian knots of his
cramped diction. I think that if I had not, as an inveterate porch
sitter, seen for myself the spangle that sunlight filtered through
limbs and leaves throws on a narrow-boarded floor, I would be
unable to untangle this complexity. Yet once the whole image is
glimpsed, the surface meaning comes away easily, each word as
succinct and tightly fitting as a cuff button.

Her compounds are not confined to modifiers. Taylor loves
to fuse separate nouns into single words, making integral images
out of discrete parts. I am reminded a little of the musical practice of tone clusters when she denominates the look on a young
man's face as "Kiss-me-quick-I'm-off-goodbye" in "Diary Entry,
March 24." In "A Change of State," a certain stage of the growth
of a flower is "a yes-but-little-lower-than." The surprising quality of her nouns is secured not only by compound formations;
the wittiness in "A Place Apart" of calling a bishop's house "an
alleluia on a rock" is patent and in "Wind" the choice of "disattendance" instead of "absence" is a lovely, subtle distinction. I
have chosen for my favorite the adjective-and-noun compound

phrase in "Hatchways" as the aptest description of Eleanor Taylor's poetry: "some not-as-yet-known electrothought."
Some of her compounds are not highly remarkable; "faceshells" in "Playing for the Funeral" and "girlskin" in "No" might have been furnished by any number of bright poets, but no one else would ever have come up with this one word she uses to describe the opulence a woman enjoys who has rented a richly furnished house that she cannot easily afford. She goes leisurely through a stranger's treasures here and the house is her—*Alibabaiad.*

Is it fair to suggest that a certain stubbornness may motivate such peculiarities? I can easily imagine this poet having to debate with editors, especially with copy editors, persuading them to allow to stand a verb like "phobe" in "Casting About." To swim lazily on one's side in a pond is to imitate the action of the water lily, but did no editorial eyebrows frown, or at least elevate, at the adverb "lilily" in "Goodbye Family"? If argument was offered against these oddities, Taylor prevailed. She hints at her aesthetic reasons in a little verse called "Stet." In poetry she prefers the flower, the "not-as-yet-known electrothought," to the complete articulation, the pupa ("nymph") to the full-blown splendor:

> I can't like the butterfly.
> I liked my nymph
> Lack-locomotive
> Descintillate
> Maleloquent.
> But the lines flutter off
> In clacking print.

Yet what I have called stubbornness may actually be a kind of modesty, the reserve that finds more meaning, more power in the incomplete utterance than in the finished poem. There are some of us who prefer, say, the pencil drawings and oil sketches of John Constable to his big varnished canvases that for all their magniloquence lack some of the rub of personality that the less finished works show.

But whether modest or stubborn, there is an insistent, contrarious impulse in Taylor's poetry and one way it manifests itself is in a purposeful, though decorous, violation of tone. When Allen Tate referred to her as a "formalist," he didn't mean that she employs fixed forms. In fact, she mostly avoids them. He was talking about a certain stringency of thought and circumspection of tone. Taylor is not a poet who will indulge in slang or descend into obscenity; her useful violations undercut the sophistication of diction and conceit with sudden, though not furtive, irruptions into old-fashioned "country" usages. Sometimes the effect is just as tonic as if she had used a slang word or whispered a cuss word. One of my favorites is when in "Woman as Artist" she describes some tulips as "dark," some as "light," and some as "streakèdy."

"Streakedy" is a word I hadn't come across since my excessively rural childhood until I read this poem. It was usually applied to the sidemeat of a hog: "streakedy bacon." Taylor's background is rural, too, or small-town enough to count as rural. That is why she is able, in speaking of a woman's purse, to conjure up the accuracy of "harness creak of shoulder bag" ("The Painted Bridge"). That's why, in "Buck Duke and Mamma," she can refer to food as "rations" and to the meat of the walnut as its "goody" in "Cousin Ida." That's why she can report the law-abiding chain gang guard as wishing he had "learned to tear-up-jack" ("The Chain Gang Guard"). And though usages like these are often put into the voices of rural personae who would use them naturally, the other diction in the poems is more formal, less distinctively "country," so that these instances stand out. A particularly savory example occurs in "How He Returned Thanks," where children listen to tiresome table graces with "squinched-up ears."

Taylor is familiar with rural customs and tasks and this familiarity makes a verb like "grabbled" the inevitable choice in "Daymother with Forks": "The long-handled potato fork/grabbled underground/when flowers came." Anyone who has ever set boot sole to potato fork knows that "grabbled" is the best word to describe the exploratory action of the broad tines as they lift below, then plunge up and out of the soil, with a muffled, wholesome, tearing sound. It is the perfect verb.

Verbs, verbs, verbs—they are the weakness of most poets who will use pallid and even passive constructions in order to push on toward the lusciousness of their modifiers. Puny verbs like *is, seem, become, have, change,* and so forth lie on the pages like dabs of library paste and serve mainly the same purpose; they are only a glue that holds the other, easier, parts of sentences together. Taylor's poems break this norm violently. As regards diction, her best strength is in her verbs, and this aspect of her work points toward an intensity of focus, a confidence of claimancy, that few other poets achieve. Again, the names of Dickinson and Hopkins come to mind; like Taylor, these poets delight in seizing with equal eagerness the thorn along with its rose.

Not all her verbs are entirely idiosyncratic. One can imagine e. e. cummings describing a poet revising lines as someone who "unwords poems" ("A Place Apart"). Another poet might come up with a tintype "glassing" in the drawer ("Lucinda Comes to Visit"). Another southern poet might say of a year that it "gallivants/across the newborn moor" ("Roulette").

It is not always lack of invention that waters down a poet's verbs. Sometimes it is lack of courage, obeisance to some vague tacit rule of contemporary literary propriety. A less venturesome poet than Taylor might reject the verb in "The passion flower/irrays out its nails" on the ground that "irrays" is strained and disrupts the tenor of the poem. And this might be true if the rest of "The Altar Needlework" lacked knotty musculature—but it doesn't.

She loves to transfer functions, making nouns and adjectives into verbs. In "The Bine Yadkin Rose," "Miss Bine taught one to violet the wrists," that is, to wear an unobtrusive bracelet of flowers. My best dictionary lists no verb form, "to stodge," so I surmise that Taylor's usage is a back formation from the adjective: "The cars that pass us eye us curiously—/Stodged with our

eyes, our frozen triggers cocked" ("The Chain Gang Guard").
Another back formation, from the nouns "descendants" and "ascendants," bestows Taylor with one of her outrageous puns:
"Bury the ladder and scend no more." ("One Not Descended").

"Whippoorwill" is one of her subtlest poems; its central conceit is that trying to pin down the ineffable but inescapable influence of the memory of an ancestor upon oneself is like trying to glimpse the loud-voiced but evasive whippoorwill. Finally the speaker of the poem, after hearing the bird for a long time, does catch sight of it, and this incident causes her to have faith that "that grandmother past knowing" was an actual person and not just a ghostly fictive memory. She addresses the bird:

> That's what I get for believing
> in your voodoo.
> You are real. She is, too.
> I've backed the hour.

In these final lines, the pun underscores the theme: The poet has been able, with the aid of the whippoorwill, to return to time past, to "back" the hour in the sense of "backing it up," and so she now supports ("backs") the truth she has found there.

I am not convinced that this is a successful use of her usual technique; this particular pun feels flimsy to me. But then I'm not certain that I've read the poem correctly either; its theme is as elusive as the bird that serves as its central symbol.

Such uncertainty is not unusual for me in reading the poems of Eleanor Ross Taylor. My perplexities most often proceed from my ignorance of history and of the poet's biography. More than a few poems seem extremely private in their references, sometimes even in their intentions. But there are lines, and a few whole poems, that puzzle me because I cannot tease clear meanings from the phrases. It is not my purpose here merely to confess my shortcomings; I'd like to believe that some of my puzzlement is caused by the poet's aesthetic principles. The ideal that she proposes in "Stet" of the incompletely formed poem as being superior in power and suggestiveness to the finished poem in "clacking print" is bound to bring about some measure of confusion in even the most scrupulous readers.

It is this aesthetic that makes necessary her dependence upon the strong, multi-purposed verb form. It is the ideal that gives us "those relics atticked/in your head" in "To Future Eleanors" and "blank ice radaring through the walls" in "May Freeze." It gives us "layer" as a verb in "Sparrow Eats Fried Chicken Wing" and "vortexed" as a modifier in "A Place Apart." It is the principle that makes possible two perfect verbs in a single construction in "Waking at Night in a New Apartment": "A sixteen-wheeler wallops by, drubbing the walls."

Do I have a candidate for the most outré verb in Taylor's work? Well, several, in fact, but I lean most acutely toward the description of a pair of world travelers who have "Kiplinged past Chinese bandits" in "The Searchers." I admire the image of a young man sitting late in a bar, drinking beer and discussing intellectual and literary topics as "amberizing Freud and Philip Levine/with his friends." But that verb is perfect only in its justness and is not as adventurous as some others—not as adventurous as, say, shadows "crocheting" together widely separated ceiling lights in "Maternity Ward." One remarks with astonishment the absent needlework artisan who "mollusks somewhere" in "The Altar Needlework," but I am also partial to the coinage that suggested the title of this essay, the noun-turned-adjective that for me so swiftly and neatly denotes the most evident quality of Taylor's lines. In "Going, Dark" she describes a woman waiting for the death of her husband in a hospital ward; the both of them know that he will perish when night falls. He is so weakened that he is resigned to the inevitability, but she realizes that his death will not be a final solution for her; her sorrows and duties and responsibilities will now increase. *"I'm not through with it yet . . ."* she thinks, while her nails "bite at her voltaged flesh."

Any poetic idiom that employs such special means will have fairly narrow confines. It is impossible for me to imagine Emily Dickinson narrating, rather than suggesting, a story. It is fruitless fun to think of Hopkins writing *vers de société* or of Marianne Moore reporting, at length, realistic dialogue. Certain kinds of excellence exclude other kinds and in Taylor's poetry it is possible for a reader to miss a relaxed easiness. I have an impression that she would make a nifty translator of Nerval and of Hölderlin but would give us rather stiff versions of Boileau or Goethe. Intensity has its limitations.

But the rewards it offers are to be found in no other manner of writing. As much as I admire the poetry of Richard Wilbur, as many virtues as I have always found in it, I still have never been as startled there as I have been in coming across this use of personification in "A Place Apart": "Book spines soliloquize, they/beckon explorations with a map." Even more surprising is this one in "The Hostage": "Answerlessness is a fence/in a film war." Or maybe this one in "Limits": "What's unsaid lacks ears."

Of course, I really wouldn't want to see such constructions in poems by Wilbur or Philip Larkin or William Meredith or Mary Oliver. These usages can occur only in poems whose textures they would not distress, in poems where a sense of strain is a necessary element of their idiom. Taylor's poems are mannerist in the same way that certain of Richard Crashaw's and many of Abraham Cowley's are. They transgress the bounds of ordinary proprieties while still maintaining a strong modesty of intention.

A spendthrift man swapped a jacket for a banjo to which he "yo-lee-lay-hoed . . ./on front steps at dusk" ("These Gifts"). Future Eleanor Taylors, cut off from traditional roots and a country background, will belong to "the sacrileged class" ("To Future Eleanors"). A man lying in a coma is caught up in a "semidormant,/nightclothes, saw-toothed dream" ("Cocoon"). "Impounding and freeing the companions" — that's a taxi cab doing its job ("Rack and Ruin").

These examples, which could be many times multiplied, are little jolts of "voltaged" language; they are "electrothought." In speaking of the poems of Eleanor Ross Taylor I have been forced to wrest with unmannerly violence her own terms from their contexts. My improprieties are regrettable, but I have found them necessary — and do so again even as I repeat my transgressions. Her term "shutterflux" describes pointedly her moments of special intensity. Perhaps this time my sin is only venial and not cardinal, for the poet applies the noun herself to the first twinge of creative impulse in "On the Writing of Poems":

I want that shutterflux
that in the morning is
the light tax
that's its own scrip:
that pays me for the smell
of bacon in the frying pan,
defrays all day
a dying capital.

2.

I have been looking at separate examples of Taylor's diction, a word or two at a time, but a poem has to be a whole, an integral object. One of the difficulties this poet has to face is the problem of making wholes, of preventing parts of her diction from becoming each a separate "shutterflux" and thus disrupting so forcefully the flow that a poem fails to hold together. If Taylor's art is a sort of verbal macramé in which the knots are designed to show, her macramés still have to be whole works; their main interest cannot be in the discrete knots themselves but in how they are woven together.

To this end, some of the lines must be less dense, less "voltaged," than others. Most of her poems, especially the longer pieces, will have certain highly charged nexuses and the language that connects these will be more relaxed, less clenched than the particularly dense passages. In other words, the work cannot be made up entirely of knots; some lengths of string have to remain unknotted.

For purposes of illustration I've chosen "Hatchways" because it deals, in fairly direct fashion, with the usage of the not fully formed thought. This poem begins with a brief account of a dream, or of two related dream episodes, in which an ill-defined passageway opens upon a sudden wide vista:

Sleeping rapidly
I climb desperately
a hatchway mercilessly
narrow-chambered. . . .
or else a slimy chimneypot

> my toehold crumbling
> as I twist up
>
> that offers
> (if I get through)
>   a fatal ledge
> hung over deluged plains,
> no roads there, sea snapping—

The first three lines end with urgent adverbs, the poet introducing immediately a tone of anxiety. The fourth line ends with an ellipsis which offers a very brief respite from this claustrophobic anxiety; those three periods serve the same purpose that a dissolve in a film sequence serves because the following lines offer an alternative vision to help explain the speaker's feeling of entrapment. It seemed at first a hatchway, but now it becomes a chimney through which she struggles. Once she comes through this narrow passage, the scene is that of a "deluged plain"; it is not a seascape but rather a landscape overwhelmed by flood, a dangerous place.

The next stanza is transitional. The speaker wonders about the origin of the dream. It might be an ordinary birth-trauma visitation, but she rejects this idea. Why should she be haunted by birth trauma? She has been told that her coming into the world was an easy passage:

> Where did this terror come from?
> this twitching like despair?
> I whose birth was
> "the easiest one"
> who came fast and simply—I
> have no need for such nightmares.

The poem began with alternative choices—hatchway or chimneypot—and it pursues this strategy in the final four stanzas, as the speaker ponders different possible explanations or the origin of her dream. Each of them is strange and fantastic, but there is no indication that she does not consider all of them serious possibilities.

The first is that she has been visited by the dying experience of a drowned sailor. Asleep, her mind is immersed in the infinite sea of the collective unconscious and is receptive to the other minds present there. Perhaps her dream is the sailor's final lament:

> Did some drowned sailor
> drifting in race memory, on
> some not-as-yet-known electrothought,
> chance up in me,
> rebuking his hard fate?

The term "electrothought," like other terms in this poem, is ambiguous. It may mean—as I have proposed above—a kind of unformed intimation of a thought, a "twitching" of the psyche; or "electrothought" may refer to a message received from another psyche, a kind of mental telegram and the compound adjective, "not-as-yet-known," may refer to the idea that science has not yet discovered and described this phenomenon. In the latter case, there is an implication that at a later date, scientists will find out about "electrothought." It is likely that Taylor intends for both meanings to be held in mind.

She offers another possible explanation for the dream's origin. Perhaps it is the voice of an unhappy ancestor who needs to tell his tale, to make known his presence in the psyche of the speaker. This miserable forefather, this "wretch," desires for the speaker to acknowledge his influence upon her personality:

> Or some wretch in my family past,
> too far back for my tale-tellers
> to reach back to, come navigate
> my sleep,
> and wring his trauma out?
> rise jinni in my blood?
> say that he's me?

In the two stanzas we have read, the speaker serves as a listener; her function is to hear the sailor's dying lament or to recognize that a long-dead ancestor contributes to her personality, that he is a part of herself. In both cases, the voices she hears demand that their lives be known, that their historical presences in the world be remarked. They belong to the past, but they struggle against being erased by the passage of time.

The next two voices belong to the future. If the past desires not to be forgotten, the future desires that its apprehensions be known and acknowledged in present time. Adrift in the collective sea, the speaker's mind may be receiving a message from her unborn grandchild, swimming in its private yet correspondent ocean, two hundred miles distant from where she sits:

> Or is that
> soon-to-be-born
> blood of my blood,
> two hundred miles away,
> gathering his-or-her strength
> (mixed with mine)
> on the private, drowsy
> sea of amnion,
> something like thought
> disturbing its red cobweb:
> > *No choice now.*
> > *Only the job that all flesh must —*
> he-or-she summoning
> our strength for being hurled
> through the dread channel to
> the raw bite of the world?

Of the possible explanations the poem offers for the origin of the dream, this one seems at first the most likely, the most "natural." The grandmother's dream is caused by anxiety about the birth of her grandchild; she has been concerned about the welfare of mother and child and in her dream she takes the role of the baby, trying to endure its birth pangs for it.

Yet the fetus does not seem frightened. The tone of its message is one of resignation; being born is only an arduous task it must somehow get through: *"No choice now./Only the job that all flesh must —."* Its purpose in communicating is to draw strength from the grandmother to aid in its passage through "the dread channel."

The final possible voice that may have called up the dream is strangest of all. Perhaps the person the speaker hears is herself, her future identity which shall be reincarnated in a lineal descendant. This descendant will be unaware of the speaker's presence and the speaker, in this hypothetical future, shall be trying to make herself known to the mortal being that encloses her. The situation will be as stifling and claustrophobic as the hatchway or chimney-pot passageway because the descendant will be too obtuse — "deaf, stubborn" — to be aware of the speaker:

> Or a black foreshadow
> of my shade,
> me waking blind
> inside strange blood
> next century,
> mute,
> laboring to get the ear
> of some deaf, stubborn,
> all-enclosing metamorph:
> I'm here, here   ?

My term "reincarnation" is inaccurate. Someone reincarnated as another person at a later date is that person. But the speaker in this case shall be only a deeply submerged part of the descendant's personality. And I have taken another liberty, supposing the future envelope for the speaker's identity to be a descendant. The poem does not say so and, given the notion that an unknown sailor's voice may have triggered the dream, the poet's future submerged self may actually be speaking inside the mind (or blood) of someone who is no kin to her.

I have taken these momentary liberties because it is so difficult to lay out in clear prose the shape of the poet's fancy. The final stanza surely embodies one of the most fantastic notions I have ever seen in poetry; it is a conceit worthy of the most refined of the Metaphysical poets, this notion that a dream of suffocating enclosure may be a cry of agony from one's own future ghost which finds itself trapped in an unresponding personality. It is a terrifying possibility and the poem ends with a desperate plea for recognition: "I'm here, here   ?"

I take the triple space between the third word and the question mark as a representation of the future self's ghostly, wan, wistful dying away. This visual cue is in line with Taylor's frequent practice of using a pun to close with (*here*   *?* = *hear?*). There are other puns, too, such as "foreshadow/of my shade," and the title of the poem alludes to the birth canal, the way one is "hatched" into the world. But the puns are not insisted upon; the interest of the language lies in Taylor's ingenious verbal intensity, in her extreme compression and multifoliate suggestiveness.

I would remark, though, that the second stanza and the final one lack that patented intensity. In these passages the diction— except for "all-encompassing metamorph" in the penultimate line—is, if not ordinary, still straightforward and easily accessible. The reason is that the second stanza serves as transition from the description of the dream to the main thread of the poem, four different speculations as to the possible origin of the dream. The final stanza is couched in a more relaxed idiom, probably because the oddity of the poet's conception demanded an open clarity for its comprehensible articulation. In these latter lines the conception itself supplies the energy that Taylor often locates in her diction.

3.

Taylor conceives of the mind of the speaker of "Hatchways" as an individual entity, aware of its individuality and defending it. It is located in some sort of medium that allows it to receive messages, dim and imperfect ones, from other minds. It cannot recognize the identities of other minds, nor can it be certain of the intentions behind the messages it receives. At the same time, the speaker's mind can desire to transmit messages but cannot know whether it has succeeded and cannot guess how its messages would be interpreted if they were received. (I have a half-formed image in my head of great numbers of electric eels swimming in a murky ocean, continually emitting bursts of energy, sensing blindly the presences of each other. It is a picture vaguely but genuinely disturbing.)

The difficulties in interpreting these dream messages are caused by the fact that the identities of those who transmit them are uncertain and because the moments of contact are so fleeting and tentative. And since the messages travel through time as well as through space the signals are bound to be distorted to some degree.

All these ambiguities, then, are the germinators of the poem. On the face of it, the poem is highly personal: "Let me tell you about my dream." But it develops that the poem is, in fact, impersonal because the dream does not proceed from the speaker's own mind but is received from elsewhere, from blood relation or stranger or future ghost. This mind is continually receiving "not-as-yet-known electrothought," wisps and whispers and spectral laments and receding fearful moans, and these almost imperceptible nudges from outside the poet's psyche are the suggestions that give rise to poems.

Because the messages received are faint, they must be amplified—and that function belongs to the intense diction. Phrases like "*wring* his trauma out," "red *cobweb*," "*raw bite* of the world," "sea *snapping*," and "*rise jinni* in my blood" [my emphases] may seem exotic, eccentric, and even awkward upon occasion, but they are necessary to bring into realization those subdued, vague scraps of communication the mind has received. These phrases are rather like transducers that convert one sort of energy to another; in this case, the received "electrothought" is converted into language, somewhat in the way that a microphone converts sound into electrical impulse.

That is why I have borrowed a term from "Going, Dark" to describe the language of Taylor's poetry; it is "voltaged." Its prickly intensity may be regarded as a form of hyperbole. The hints the mind picks up from outside are magnified by the poet's diction; that is the vital spark that brings the poem into being. Many poets are admired for the justness and propriety of their diction and one could not desire the lines of Elizabeth Bishop or Edward Thomas to be different from what they are. But voltaged language is rare and, for me, uniquely exciting. It is one of the greatest pleasures of reading Eleanor Ross Taylor.

Behind "The Altar Needlework"

In September, 1988, the Taylors and I visited Westover Church and its altar needlework, which Eleanor Ross Taylor was soon (in *Days Going / Days Coming Back*) to draw into one of her finest poems.

Peter Taylor was scheduled for an appearance at Rappahannock Community College in Warsaw, a small town in Virginia's Northern Neck. There was to be a screening of *The Old Forest*, a film adapted from his short story; since Peter had recently suffered a stroke, and Eleanor has never driven, I readily agreed to drive.

On the way home the following day, we made a short detour to the old river road which parallels the James between Williamsburg and Richmond. The gently winding highway affords glimpses of grand plantation houses; immense fields stretch towards the river. Tree branches meet overhead.

Five miles west of Charles City Courthouse, we came to Westover Church, surrounded by huge trees and a cemetery from the far side of which you can see Herring Creek—wide enough, at this point, to be mistaken for the river. Parishioners are still being buried in the cemetery, but you can also find markers like the broken-off stone of Richard Weir, Merchant, who died "17 June 1748 . . . of his age the 25th year."

Built in 1730, the church was used as a barn when the Episcopal Church fell into disfavor after the Revolutionary War. Revived in the 1830s, it again saw hard times when Federal troops used it as a stable during the Civil War. It has always been associated with the families of the nearby plantations, the Harrisons of Berkeley and the Carters of Shirley. Several presidents have worshipped there. A silver chalice dating from 1695 is one of its treasures.

A charming aspect of the church's interior is the intricate embroidery decorating the lectern, the kneeling cushions for the altar rail, and the kneeling cushions for the acolytes. There are raccoons, rabbits, dogwoods, daffodils and dragonflies; one piece even features the tracks of animals and birds. The needlework brings to mind Paul's statement in *Romans* that God's "invisible nature, namely His eternal power and deity, has been clearly perceived in the things that have been made."

Some time later, Eleanor wrote me that her poem, "The Altar Needlework," had been inspired by our visit. The embroiderer ". . . sits in a family room/on Herring Creek,/in front of Nature or/Your Wild America. . . . " Her renderings of plants and creatures are mentioned, along with the toll the close work has taken: "She used her eyes up,/these envisaging:/the pepper on the robin's chin,/the minnow's slippy scales,/egg pollen on the bee's foot."

There is a beautiful interplay between the artist, the things she's created, and the act of creation itself. There is also the climactic shift in perspective in which God is imagined as the embroiderer, making the woman who made the art: "He/snipped her off/and cut her out/and wove her thus/a small and female thing/blue eyed, fine fingered. . . ."

During a visit in Charlottesville in December, 1999, Mrs. Taylor told me that she considered this one of her best poems.

Ѳ Ѳ Ѳ

When asked to contribute to this volume, I decided to return to Westover Church.

It was a beautiful sunny day, not that cold for January. Julia Boyd, a vestry person at the church, had put me in touch with her mother-in-law, Mary Archer Boyd. Mary Boyd, along with Helle Carter, of nearby Shirley plantation, were the two most responsible for the church's needlework.

"It started in 1975 when Mrs. Albert Copland died," said Boyd. A vigorous 87, she is much more outgoing than the artist I'd imagined in Taylor's poem. "Mrs. Copland was a hardworking lady for the church, an old, old member, from the generation ahead of me. This little church has sort of been carried on by people who just take over and *do*. So when she died we wanted to do something special, not just send flowers."

The project took shape following visits to the National Cathedral in Washington, D.C., and several Richmond-area churches. "We saw what they had, then we did our own thing.

"What we really went for was to have symbols that were Christian, that was top of the list." Followed by nature and history. "We had the creek and we had the flowers. You'd be amazed at how many flowers there are. We had all of those things, so it was a shame not to utilize them.

"We just wanted to be Charles City, be this church."

Boyd showed me the four kneelers for the altar rail. Their designs are based on the four seasons. A herring is the centerpiece for spring. The fish's upstream migration signals the end of winter, and gave the creek its name. "And of course the herring is an old, old Christian symbol. Fishes have always stood for Christianity." The herring is surrounded by renderings of the spring-blooming dogwood, tulip poplar and redbud. Each of the four cushions took a year to complete.

"These are for the children," said Boyd, indicating the acolyte kneelers behind the altar. They are decorated with a deer, a raccoon, a rabbit, and a very large goose. "The children are all hunters down here."

Boyd showed me the hanging for Trinity, roughly summer and fall: three catfish swim against a background of animal tracks; the outside border is a frame of twelve insects. "The catfish, that come right out of the James River, represent the Trinity; the paws are for the animals on the earth, the insects for the air."

This is my favorite of all the needlework at Westover. It is playful, arresting, and uniquely reverent. Something of its spirit is in "The Altar Needlework"; on reflection, I realized that it had indeed been on display when we visited the church.

"That's what we've done," said Boyd. She sat down in a pew. "It doesn't look like a lot, does it?"

She spoke about the alterations that were made when the church was rebuilt following the Civil War. "They were trying to make a big church out of a little country church. The interior of the church is all wrong."

Bright winter sunlight streamed in through the windows. It suddenly struck me that stained glass, rather than needlework, would have been the more conventional route for memorials. "Weren't we lucky!" she said. "They didn't have enough money. Oh, weren't we lucky! Now you can look out, watch the squirrels and the birds and the bees.

"No," said Boyd with finality. "Nobody wants stained glass windows in here."

Alfredo Franco

Notes On *Wilderness of Ladies*

I

Eleanor Ross Taylor's *Wilderness of Ladies* is a particularly unified collection of poems. Not a poetic sequence, the book rather recalls a novel, or, closer to the medium of poetry, a short story cycle, such as *Winesburg, Ohio*, in the recurrence of its themes and voices. As in the case of Anderson's stories, each poem in this book retains its independence, its unique poetic adventure, even while contributing to a whole.

I would like to explore some of these recurring motifs and characters. My interest is not merely to show consistency across the poems but to understand the book as such, as a cohesive document that speaks powerfully of the struggle of the individual within societal, familial, and gender-based expectations. For if many of these poems take place in the realm of Southern gentility, it is from there precisely that they cry out and mount their campaign against it—with housewifely scissors, table knives, garden shears and a devastatingly strong iambic line. Against it? Yes, but also *for* it, recognizing that it is the source of much beauty, too—the source of the poetry and its tensions, the source of great delicacies of phrase and of idiomatic richness, and most importantly, the spur to memory.

II

The tension is already in the title. A wilderness is a solitary, uncultivated place, while ladies are a form of human cultivation. But wilderness can have other meanings. The word can indicate an ornamental garden or park, nature at its *most* cultivated, and indeed, acts of gardening abound in *Wilderness of Ladies*. A wilderness can also be an allegorical labyrinth where one easily loses one's moral way—the narrator of "The Pilgrim's Progress" calls the whole world "the wilderness." The ladies and their world form a wilderness through which the "I" wanders and from which it often seeks, in vain, to escape. *The Oxford English Dictionary* tells us that a wilderness can be "a mingled, confused, or vast assemblage or collection of persons or things." The *O.E.D.* goes on to illustrate this meaning with a line from Shakespeare that recalls startlingly the title of Ms. Taylor's book: "Dost thou not perceive that Rome is but a wilderness of tigers?" (*Titus Andronicus*, iii.i. 54).

But what, really, is a lady? She is, the *O.E.D.* says, "a woman whose manners, habits and sentiments have the refinement characteristic of the higher ranks of society." Yet at the root of the word *lady* is less a refined woman than a woman at work. *Hlaefdig*, the Old English source of lady, means to knead bread. Housework is a theme in *Wilderness of Ladies* and idleness is relentlessly feared, lest the house and garden become

A spot where idle birds whet idle bills.

Housework may be the bane of the ladies, but it might also be why they are at the source of poetry, of memory. As Gaston Bachelard wrote in *The Poetics of Space*: "Through housewifely care a house becomes not so much its originality as its origin."

III

Wilderness of Ladies is, among other things, a gallery of women. Some of the women are oppressed, some oppressive; some are rebellious, some are liberated through art; some cast their spell from beyond life itself. Some are ladies, some are ghosts, and some are tigers. Among them are the "flaxseed aunts" who reprimand the "I" in "Wind" for believing in a beloved phantom; there is Miss Bine, who tries to cultivate the indomitable Miss Tempe; there is Miss Hattie Yow, the elocution teacher, and poor Mrs. Presterling who "revised/a spontaneity" in the new house in "Moved." There are the ladies who "crack nuts and ice cubes" in the parlor in "Goodbye Family"; there is the weary narrator in "Sister" with the errands in her lap and dreams of escape. Of course, overseeing the book, is the

"Woman as Artist," the toughest "lady" of all, heir of Miss Tempe and, like her, a mother. She asserts, in language leaner than any other in the book:

> I'm mother.
> I hunt alone.

IV

Wilderness of Ladies is a book that is full of oppositions: cultivation (societal and horticultural) versus naturalness; the desire to escape versus a sense of inaction; the ever-present house versus the freedoms and dangers outside; childhood versus adulthood (especially in that most haunting poem, "Playing"); the "I" versus the family, versus the ladies, versus itself.

Pervasive throughout the whole book is the *melding* of past and present, currency and memory, the living and the dead into one voice:

> In two spots time and timeless both live
> Companions —
> — "Escape"

Finally, there are ghosts and passages of graveyard poetry, which when added to the centrality of the house lend the book a distinct Gothic character. First, let us look at the issue of cultivation versus nature.

V

The opening poem, "The Bine Yadkin Rose," introduces this opposition of cultivation and naturalness. The poem begins in an act of horticultural grafting that will soon become societal. The grafting of wild and garden roses will give way to the attempt to "cultivate" a spirited young woman, Miss Tempe, by an old spinster, Miss Bine.

Grafting is a unifying process that involves separation, cutting. It is an amputation from the original root. The mournful opening lines emphasize the paradox of successful grafting as a form of orphanhood and divorce:

> Bemiracled rose, I see my cutting took:
> Sad horn, the spell-rocked cradle of a rose —
> Look! how the foster brier grows
> That mother bed, that lover bed forsook.

The book thus begins with cutting, and will abound throughout in sharp implements. At one point, in the poem "Flesh and Spirit," the domestic scissors will take on the role of a pioneer's machete clearing the wilderness:

> Like scissors whacking the vegetation
> To the side, to the front

And in the poem "Goodbye Family" the "I" will ask:

> Every day I opened the drawer and
>   Scanned the knives;
> Were there enough, sharp enough,
>   For all lives?

Miss Tempe, whose name resonates with rhythm and time, goes to sew for Miss Bine. What should function for Miss Tempe as a finishing school, a grafting of refinement onto her, ends rather in a "raggy scrapbag pantomime" of refinement. The cutting doesn't quite take. In the third stanza of "The Bine Yadkin Rose," she speaks indiscreetly to a gentleman:

> "I accuse you, Mr. Stapleton,
> Of excess temperance — ha-ha!"
> "Miss Tempe . . . I beg . . . Allow me to insist —!"

The irreverence is typical of Miss Tempe, who in another poem, "Cousin Ida," will exclaim, upon hearing of Uncle Wylie's death: "You ought t've been gone from here long ago!" In yet another poem, "Buck Duke and Mamma," Miss Tempe is glad that the character Buck Duke lacks excess temperance. She likes that he "had a devilish eye," for

It saved an orphan from dire fortitude,
And saved his grandpa's house from sanctity.

Miss Tempe will have none of the histrionics of ladyship and is always spiritedly on the side of naturalness, against cultivation. Taking up her scissors (by now a familiar implement in the book), she prunes her garden of excess and artificiality. After the death of Buck Duke

The histrionic garden did not bear
One saucy pose when she put down the scissors. . . .

In "The Bine Yadkin Rose" (that impossible graft of Miss Bine and Miss Tempe), parenthetical couplets at the end of three of the stanzas further convey the conflict of artifice versus nature:

The artful rose of stiff, dispiteous stem
Blenched lest a natural beauty should offend.

Miss Bine's cultivation cannot mask her loneliness. She enacts a pantomime of her own, an imaginary marriage:

Unringed, but wed, she took a ring and wed
Unwed. . . .

Near death, she seems to confide to someone — perhaps to Miss Tempe — the true sterility of her life and of the quotidian household existence of women:

Move into a house that's not yet built,
And there's scant time to prune a rose and spray.
You dish potatoes up three times a day,
And put your wedding dress into a quilt.

It is no wonder that Miss Tempe later, an adult mother, will be less than fanatical about her household work while at the same time mocking another melodramatic, yet clearly beloved lady:

As she went about her cast-off household chores
She overlooked them with a lavish bow
Inspired by that heroine of poems,
Her elocution teacher, Miss Hattie Yow.

— "Buck Duke and Mamma"

At the end of "The Bine Yadkin Rose," the "I" of the poem is careful not to breed too artificial a flower:

Nor color up, just barely cultivate;
An austere blossom for each Sunday plate. . . .

In one of the most moving of the poems, "Wind," a young woman, Gabriella, seems to escape cultivation and find strength, life itself, only in death. The "I" sees her walking out in the windy night. She has shed her lady-likeness. She is now "barefoot and mudfouled," yet also seems "with strength grown bodywise." The "I" no longer recognizes the signs of Gabriella's cultivation:

And wherever the dreamy, cultivated
Part of her had fled to—
It was not in her ghost, nervous, human eyes
I kept seeing.

(It is interesting to note that cultivation, for all its sterility, is here associated with reverie, and so conducive to the poetic act.) The vision is both frightening and welcome to the "I," who commands her to "howl"—a mournful yet loud, unladylike expression.

In this poem, too, we see the desire to escape hindered by a decay of the will—one of the consequences, perhaps, of cultivation. The poem's narrator, a young lady, living in the gloomy "knifestruck disattendance" (another cutting image) in the wake of Gabriella's death, has lost her dynamism:

And it was no use looking for anything,
In the cupboards, or out the door.
Long ago, something had eaten out my marrow. . . .

She is still able to yearn, but only for the past:

> And I was hungry now, for years before.

The dead Gabriella seems more alive than the trapped narrator. The narrator in the poem "Sister" contemplates, if for a brief moment, an escape from her cultivated existence. The narrator begins by recalling the sibling with whom she survived the stresses of family life:

> The wars of marriage and the family burst around us.

It is with this sister, however, that the "I" explored the past, embodied in the "old-house place," to which the path—the path of time and memory—is "washed out . . . but not erased." But more than the mysterious past was explored in her company: nature, too, a wilderness, was shared, and perhaps even a degree of sexual knowledge was attained in tandem:

> Then we discovered within the close
> Our exotic properties, our pretty price.

There is an Edenic feeling to the world that the sisters shared, Eden the original wilderness and the Paradise Lost (Milton Street!), while the very sun watches them like some elder who has espied two young nymphs in Arcady:

> The sun that baked our mud-bread
> Hides slyly in the trees
> Between Spring Garden and Milton Streets
> And howls at what we eat.

The sister was a comrade in the exciting world of the uncultivated. In the last stanza of the poem, the "I," adult now, yearns for a similar comrade, for a moment of respite from the demands of cultivation and family life:

> And riding the trolley homeward this afternoon
> With the errands in my lap

> I would have disfestooned my world —
> A husband, more or less!
> A family, more or less! —
> To have alighted to a cup of kettle-tea
> And someone
> To whom I could lie merrily,
> Use malapropisms, be out-of-taste. . . .

The narrator feels her incompleteness without the sister and dreams of union — a kind of grafting:

> We'd play it solitary while the dusks rushed by,
> More than one flesh-and-blood,
> Almost one I.

In "Goodbye Family," the "I" envisions an escape from the familial house and its gentility, a house in which "ladies crack nuts and ice cubes," and where it foresees its ineffectual future

> Clanging and pacing in the rooms
> Of next year.

The vision or dream of escape involves what Bachelard calls a "house . . . imagined as a vertical being." The "I" falls through the verticality of the house:

> To cut free
> And drop through the cloak closet and cellar
> Is better —
> Under the foundations of God's world. . . .

"Verticality," Bachelard explains, "is ensured by the polarity of the cellar and attic." Bachelard attributes specific forces to this polarity: "Indeed," he writes, "it is possible to oppose the rationality of the roof to the irrationality of the cellar." For Bachelard, the cellar "is first and foremost the *dark entity* of the house, the one that partakes of subterranean forces."

In "Goodbye Family," the "I" conspires with these subterranean forces, which lead her to a state free of cultivation, where the eyes become

> . . . unlettered,
> And intellectuality an asterisk
> Now blurred —

Like a prisoner escaping from Alcatraz, the narrator must swim for life:

> And now the water
> Meeting me around the curve, roaring, blanks
> Out all but ear. . . .

This revolt against cultivation is one of the chief themes in *Wilderness of Ladies*. Interestingly, it is not only women who carry out this resistance. In the third section of the book's last poem, "Family Bible," we find that the grandfather — perhaps Miss Tempe's father? — also resists the fetters of cultivation:

> Something savage in him
> Fought civility.

Cultivation in his case is also literally impossible, sterile. He is a poor farmer with

> A hoe
> To cultivate flint rocks. . . .

In a line that recalls the "foster brier" of the book's first poem, we are told that he also must protect himself from the rose-bushes — from cultivation itself — with but

> Breeches to thwart the briers. . . .

VI

Narratives of escape, and of thwarted flight, are to be found throughout *Wilderness of Ladies*. One of the most compelling — and narrowly successful — is to be found in the poem "At the Carnival." The narrative resonates with fugitive criminality, or of fleeing slaves pursued by dogs:

> A fatal two,
> Swifting it along the king's highway. . . .
> . . . . .
> It was so cold we could only hope to hurt each other;
> Never were hands gripped harder;
> Two, skirting light and faced
> With the indicative gullets of a farmer's dogs—
> "Never let it be said we led a chase. . . .
> Drop flat."

This is also one of the very few poems in the book that takes place substantially out of the house, in a state of homelessness, yet its telling is ironically encased, housed if you will, in parentheses, as if the escape had failed after all. The narrator, the "I" is of course outside of the parentheses, not partaking of the actual escape, and must tell herself not to gaze so imploringly at the female fortune-teller who might be the object of the escape fantasy:

> Eyes, don't beseech her so!

One of the most ironic poems about escape is "The Chain Gang Guard." The guard of course is fettered to his prisoners because of his obligation to keep watch on them:

> Here I stand! Loaded gun across me—
> As if I'd get away!

In the poem "Illness," the "I" almost succeeds in escaping from the house and from life itself, but is hindered by God, napping on the porch. Encountering God, the "I" believes that it is the moment of liberating death:

> "Oh, thank you," I cried suddenly free. . . .

But God offers no such escape. He has been merely resting on the porch, aged and crying to himself, too "other-orbited" to even take notice of the narrator.

VII

As I have suggested earlier, very few of the poems in *Wilderness of Ladies* are located outside of the house. Perhaps no one has considered the role of houses in literature as thoroughly and sensitively as Gaston Bachelard in his *Poetics of Space.* "For our house," he writes, "is our corner of the world . . . it is our first universe, a real cosmos in every sense of the word." For Bachelard, the house is explored as a space of joy that encourages reverie because it is the "non-I that protects the I." In Gothic literature, however, the house is also a space of terror, entrapment, and an overwhelming embodiment of family history. Both the Bachelardian and the Gothic meanings of the house are at work in *Wilderness of Ladies.* We have seen already in several poems the Gothic oppressive feeling, the weight of family history, the need to escape, as well as the haunting by the dead. In the poem "In the Churchyard," with its resonance of the Gothic poet Gray, the new house is already weighed down with age and family memory:

> In the churchyard I hear them hammering
> On the new roof of my new house
> A hundred years old.

In the poem "Moved," a similar sense of age already pervades the new house:

> No more saying old or new; instead
> We'll dust the smiles that are discovered. . . .

A Gothic oppression also pervades the house:

> Last things close in upon us
> Like storm windows hung a week too soon.

The narrator foresees the inevitability of death and future misfortunes in the new house:

> To this address they will come,
> All the bad news of losses that must be.

> To this we desolate will come,
> Older, from our other homes.

As Bachelard writes: "An entire past comes to dwell in a new house."

Briefly, towards the end of the poem, the narrator does contemplate the future joys that may come as well:

> Will there not be liftings-up?
> Will there not be lazy breakfasts, with friends?
> Will there be births in spiraling gardens?

Yes, the poet concedes, but the concern of the poem "is of ends."

In the poem "Woman as Artist," the house is prophetic, it can answer riddles with doors like tongues:

> Did I not have some inkling of the answer,
> And the answer answered,
> The door that closed across the room
> As my door opened?

In the poem "Wind," the body of the house as it is penetrated by the wind not only figures the assault on the narrator's sense of security and self, but also stirs memories of origins:

> But the wind of a suddenly-turned season,
> Hard, and raw enough to move a solid shadow,
> Began in flaws to rush the outer closures
> And wheedle through the inner apertures . . .
> . . . . .
> I even felt my cradle agonies
> Alone, in the dark back room, revealed. . . .

The last two lines recall Bachelard when he wrote: "The house is a large cradle."

Cradle, and coffin. In the poem "Playing," this dual nature of the house is rhymed:

> The waiting womb! the waiting tomb—
> The empty antique sitting room!

Finally, there is the very Gothic poem "Night," which describes a house reminiscent of those in *Jane Eyre*:

> I spent the night in Chastelton.
> The splitting damasks hung in belts;
> Those faded colors we admired
> Forgot themselves in gray.
> Light spider-bagged the baseboards, tired.
> I climbed up to the children's room. . . .
> . . . . .
> Up steps and past a blistered stile
> Along that thick oak balustrade
> (You like old things? Behold!)

Houses, the House, predominate in the poems of *Wilderness of Ladies* to such a degree that our sense of wilderness is more as an outside presence, an ever-present threat as well as a possibility of new life; a possibility that is rarely explored, as is poignantly conveyed in "Cousin Ida":

> I, captive, cage-fond,
> Dread doors opening on the great beyond.
> . . . . .
> "Child, you'll be miserable," they warned, "Don't go."
> (Stay here where suffering's homemade, sure to fit.)

The wilderness is kept out, partly out of fear, but partly because the house itself is fascinating and irresistible even as it oppresses. It is itself a wilderness full of unknowns, or rather: full of forgottens. (All wildernesses are strangely old, in that they are the original state of things, and to discover them is actually to find the root, to re-discover.)   The ladies chart this wilderness. They are pioneers of memory. They cannot leave, they will not escape, because somebody has to remember, or the origins are lost.

The Gardener of Ghosts: Eleanor Ross Taylor's *Days Going / Days Coming Back*

Quite apart from the pensive, sensitive poets who stare at us from their enlarged and well-lit cover photos, the front of Eleanor Ross Taylor's *Days Going / Days Coming Back* sports a dense cluster of crooked tombstones. On the back there's a teeny picture of a pleasant-faced woman with a pursed mouth, and after a tolerable compliment alluding to her southernness, this sly sentence: "She writes the way a mule is said to step through tobacco rows: with a great delicacy and an unstoppable power."

But while Eleanor Ross Taylor's poetry feels the weight of land and history, the blunt burden pulled remains decisively in the human and mortal realm. Everywhere in these poems the just-dead, long-dead, and soon-to-be-dead leave their ringing mark—the days of the living the sometimes dubious gift of all those coming before, and those coming after, well, the tug of their debt to us is still to be measured. In one of the poems balancing the heaviness of death by birth, even the look at newborns and a new mother in "Maternity Ward" finishes its revery with the lines of human connection extending circularly all the way through grave and childbed: "A nurse dreams through her graveyard-shift schedule/in this time-marriage. Our flesh/delivers ghosts." The flesh has hardly arrived before it begins its descent into the past, into the already there. In a poem dedicated "To Future Eleanors," Taylor ends forebodingly by asking a presumptive grandchild:

> What will you do with
> Grandma's savings—
> those relics atticked
> in your head
> of effort, vision?
>
> On pain of death, scratch pictures
> in the dust

> as she did —
> I fear my after-thirst.

The pertinacity of the beloved dead is indeed to be feared and named. This poem is planted in a series of elegies and leave-takings, right after one in which the speaker's father says:

> I beg you, kids — no memorials, please.
> Don't write poems to me. Don't bother.
> What we said we said. What's unsaid lacks ears.

And the speaker responds, "In this I'm like my father." There doesn't seem to be an afterlife of celestial bloom to strain for yearningly, or to be crowned by poetry. One of the largest gifts of Taylor's art is to trust the plainest and most laconic of words; in "Family Bible," as "posterity" in the shape of a granddaughter, she discovers a penciled message laid away in the family clock, merely saying:

> My full name is Aminta Dunlap Watkins Ross.
> My mother was Merina Wilkerson.
> My father was Arnold Watkins — he carpentered —
> I married your pa Whitson Ross
> My wedding presents were a feather bed and two hens.

Consciousness is dynastic, but the named branches of precious descent are full of homely — "he carpentered" — and unelevated detail. Family is pervasive, but closeness is never taken for granted. A troubling portrait of the speaker's relations to her grandmother concludes "Family Bible":

> Was closeness more than painful separateness?
> We were a constellation of detached, like, ghosts.

The working of Taylor's nature is unadorned by hyperbole or hypostasis or other literary tokens of high regard; hers is nature, not Nature, and it is simply the all-pervasive medium in which we live. Any memory that outlasts death in nature is human. In "March 9" Taylor says, remarking on a burial date:

All dead hands are the same age: dead.
I note my own.
Last year, trembling,
they harvested hyacinths
for the graves' navels.
Has no one cleared away
that dessication at the stones?

Another dessication comes.

It rains. The rain is young.

Even birth and death become merely ideas that the human has breached. In the image of the graves' navels, Taylor enacts our need to mark endings and beginnings as portentous. We mourn death itself and the making of tombstones as something we are born to, dryness and aging something we are born to, while the nonhuman rains on us its random and unforced renewals. Everywhere the pressure of the human past, its power to hurt and define, is unremitting. While Taylor *does* write poems for her father, in this poetry art is not the mirror held up in which our lives may be comfortably glazed and clarified. It's as if she prefers to find her way without that hope, poetry itself only one more human dialect, the art of naming the imposition of just another order, just another stay against confusion.

The inflection is markedly southern, markedly female, and the gardening is intense, the names and practices astutely observed, as Taylor keeps tabs on all the things that feed off the ground, go into and come out of it—human, vegetable, and mineral. Largely domestic, her poems are about women, families, and interlocking generations, with occasional outreach into the territory of war and ravage into which family members may be historically brought. Appomattox, the Argonne, and Anzio are names flicked in this text or that, although Taylor's sense of the masculine heroic is severely qualified. "After Twenty Years" ends with this outburst, in the voice of a woman who mourns the death of a soldier son in these terms:

Oh the acres of undistinguished
Crosses make me sick.

> Mother could mark Papa's grave
> In the churchyard a mile from home,
> By its firs and shaft. . . .
> Your nothing grave. . . .
>   Shame!
> God I am of little understanding. . . .
> But with God all things are possible. . . .
> Give my son another life—
> A Norwood ugliness, a bourgeois rot,
> Dust and concrete, Falcons and Mustangs, not . . .

For this woman, as for other speakers, the pain of loss enters consciousness shaped as the pain of permanent exile; burial ground should properly become home ground.

Several poems bring their protagonists into Indian captivity. In "Warpaint and Camouflage," the narrative of a contemporary speaker struggling against sickness, household, and family responsibilities, braids into the experience of an earlier Indian captive. Taylor says of her earlier set of Americans:

> They were not strong on landscape,
> being captives.
> Raising the eyes and looking far
> requires a certain off-guard.
> Requires if not pleasure in, some
> concord with one's status quo.
> Mountains were never sublime and
> forests did not breathe grandeur;
> the rising sun recharged vigilance and the stars
> were reproachful for routes lost.

But even for her contemporary lot, lasting into a world in which pines have to be put in to screen out the neighbors' trash cans, and the sound haunting the primal sward is merely the suburban lawnmower, grandeur and sublimity are extraneous. The vigilant style of an earlier generation still survives in Taylor as a sober, tight-lipped economy of speech in which it is sinful to waste either words or food, and a wary rather than celebratory eye should still be kept on the weather.

In another sequence of deliberate juxtapositions, in which a historical voice modifies a contemporary one, "Rachel Plummer's Dream, Winter 1836" sits next to "In the Bitter Roots," which concludes the volume, blending Rachel's dream life into that of the poet's by the ordering of the poems. The final poem, "In the Bitter Roots," begins in Taylor's voice, as musing about Clark's earlier foray, she places herself on the near side of exploration outward:

> One who's never crossed the Mississippi
> and never will, now —
> how can I think I stand too
> in that place
> in Clark's stupendous mountains
> escape unsure
> thinking myself, too
> part of a world cut off, receding?

There is a toughness in her terse, impacted diction: you lean down and listen close, because the voice is low and often tense, and there is a tremendous sense nibbling at the edges of all the poems of leashed things not said but hinted, of assumptions made and wryly but proudly held about particular worlds of manners passing — worlds including oneself. In one short poem, comment on the life of the housewife is locked up tight, crammed into its central metaphor:

> Have pity on this little mouse
> running and hiding,
> the last mouse in the house, and
> slated, she knows, for extinction.

And yet mouse always has cat nature to contend with, or metamorphose into:

> Will mouse prowl by day,
> calling from room to room,
> her walkie-talkie loud on her belt?
> Mouse, watch it.
> You grow gross claws
> and stalk your neighbors' bassinets.

The poems glint. The description is sparse and mostly colloquial with precise, nailing verbs. Yet there's a lot of internal rhyme, of an immensely skillful but understated music of chiming vowel and consonant. An occasional stunning iambic pentameter suddenly jewels a passage of otherwise shortened lines: "The battered bees hung stupid in mid-air." Or: "The morning glories ringed the flapping corn." Or:

> Below the bridge the blue-lined buckets and
> caked lids, the wares the news was made of,
> litter the ditch's glittering careless depth.

Besides the more obvious heavy work of the booming *b*s, the littering of those *l*s, the *caked/careless*, and *ditch/depth* combos, Taylor also permits herself a humming vibrato in the short *i*, stuck to its alternating *d*s and *t*s, in *bridge, lids, litter, ditch* and *glittering*. Her pictures are always made with swift strokes: in "No," a woman's face is "a crushed girlskin," and later, "Her hair, an edgeless haze." A passenger on a bus, this woman reaches into the black plastic trash bag which is her luggage, "arm elbow deep, like one engaged in calving."

It is not a sentimental picture of birthing, or indeed of any household or garden activity, that Taylor offers. I have an idea why the jacket copy calls this poetry "sculpted": the compounds, occasionally seeming to work the words through syntactical wrenching, build up all in one unit to make a word-brick flung at reality, the fleeing target. Although a certain number of these recent poems teeter dangerously on the edge of anecdote, it's the odd angle that saves them, and an unerring accuracy that fixes them. Also a dense and unpredictable musicality, where a quickening breath startles the verbal texture into eloquence. "Boiled Peanuts" takes up a particularly southern treat, but this small poem shows how dexterously Taylor can seize a moment and flashfire it, as the roadstand servitor with "Black dress and flying hair" hands the speaker her peanuts and her ending:

> "Run out of sacks!"
> She takes a dipper
> off a monstrous hook,

tips my dank treat
into an old bread bag
and wrings it shut, then
throws my filthy bill a queasy look.

There is a pleasure in mouthing this assonance and consonance, tasting the energy of these verbs, simultaneously tucking away the shrewd glance of this poem: in this part of the world bags to "us" are sacks to "them," and a dirty bill is something many small vendors will refuse, because the abstraction of currency is not to be trusted, money still neither sign nor symbol but all too mutable thing.

Bracketed by the newer poems are poems from *Wilderness of Ladies* and *Welcome Eumenides*, her two books published originally in 1960 and 1972, respectively. I came upon these wonderfully strange, visionary poems with intense excitement when they first appeared, their polyvocal narratives in which one strains to hear the true voice like listening in to a badly tuned radio during a time of disaster, and bending to distinguish each wildly fluctuating and fragmentary broadcast. Several of the recently published poems have the same urgent, disruptive many-voicedness, although most of the newer work is a little more discursive and a shade more relaxed.

It's not too hard to account for the fierce interest of poems like "Welcome Eumenides" and "A Few Days in The South in February (A Hospitality for S.K. Wightman, 1865)." Eleanor Ross Taylor is offering us poetic narrative both lyric and heroic: the music is heightened and the themes have a thumping emotive weight. In "Welcome Eumenides" she has taken the sentimental icon, Florence Nightingale, and evaded the trivializing to which Lytton Strachey subjected her in *Eminent Victorians*, to come up with the living woman, in the freshness of her own words. Both of Taylor's dramatic monologues draw their appeal, however, from traditional moral perspectives. In "A Few Days in the South," like Anchises in search of Hector's body among the Greeks, S.K. Wightman goes to find and bury his dead son. However we may currently wish to reposition the words and events of Florence Nightingale's truly extraordinary life into feminist activism, a part of her appeal may be that however

Florence Nightingale may have reversed the Victorian sense of what it is proper for a woman to undertake, much of what she did was, if not conventional, still fully consonant with conventional ideals of female behavior. She was the protective Lady with the Lamp, virgin nursemother to the wounded soldiers of the British Army. Heroine to heroes, she paid for that achievement with wounds of her own. Taylor's accomplishment is to dodge the labeling which such a life of public service inevitably accumulates, and to retrieve from the matrix of a complex history a burning core of immediate presence. And a sense of calling, suffusing the poem's speech with the imaginative powers that this life also required:

> At last, the chance for a rich and true life.
>
> A girl, desperately fortified in my castle,
> The starched pure linen,
> Scalded plates, the sanitary air,
> The facile word killed soul-ferment.
> Six courses starved the spirit.
> *And I said of laughter, mad,*
> *And of mirth, what is it doing?*
> I dreamed of all things at man's mercy.

Each of these dramatic monologues has its peculiar pungencies and unflagging originality; in part, an earthy authenticity represented by a literal pungency. The stenches and ordures of Florence Nightingale's labor of nursing in the field hospitals of the Crimean War marry brutally with the longueurs of her upperclass breeding in England. Similarly linking the needs of the spirit and the flesh in "A Few Days in The South in February," S. K. Wightman can complete his mission to bring his son back for burial only after the providential discovery of supplies of pitch, sealing-black, and a barrel of rosin near the tidewater battlefield to which he comes to retrieve the body. It is Taylor's respect for the protrusively material, as well as the targeting accuracy of her social observation, that makes her chafed, broken utterances, her sawed-off bits of dialogue, so moving. Nothing much in contemporary poetry can touch the intensities of some of these earlier monologues, the feeling of a blaze only intermittently stifled coming off the pages. Without the polish and elegance of earlier practitioners of dramatic monologue like Browning, or of later poets like Richard Howard, her ironies are starker, blunter, more potently bitter, and full of a penetrating conviction about their worlds of suffering and glory. A brief look into one of the chaotic passages from "Welcome Eumenides" shows a few traits:

> Pen—paper—*vite*!
> They demand supplies . . .
> Ah ohhh the engine in my head. . . .
> Claret and white flour for the Persian adventurer!
>   Must I repeat:
> Do not
>   attach to the cutlets
>   (1) rags (2) nails (3) buttons
>   . . . surgical scissors
>
>   . . . that you can join me on the twenty-seventh
> (Crème Harlequin aux Meringues—or dariolettes?)
>
> And again. Please keep:
>   a. Toilets covered.
>   b. Windows open.
> Orderlies: Eat not the rations of those men asleep.
> *(The éclat of this adventure of mine!)*

Worlds jostle painfully here. Medical supplies and instruments against military despatches, orderlies against patients, high-class French dining against the desperate slops hoarded in field hospital and lazaret, even a suffocating peace-time security against the raw, open, war-time hazard, yawning dangerously like those latrines, that like the windows, admit much that is not lightly ordered or endured. Details tantalize—the mind can construct a creamy, color-blocked pudding out of Crème Harlequin aux Meringues, but "dariolettes"? They demanded the fattest and oldest dictionary in my house. But what are those cutlets, certainly not food . . . and who is "the Persian adventurer"? In the dash and tumble of this purposefully fractured space, things and people collide dangerously, ruled by that éclat—that sense of high adventure emanating from Eleanor Ross Taylor's rendering of the whole enterprise.

While Taylor's more recent poems employ the same collaging techniques, she appears to be trading in some of the dramatic momentum which she gained in these early long pieces for a quieter and more genial style. In *Days Going / Days Coming Back*, perspective shifts from being a granddaughter to being a grandmother; there are fewer poems about aunts, uncles, and a few more about friends, children, and grandchildren, where perspective shifts more to continuity than raw personal and historical rupture. There's also an alteration in her view of herself as poet. The new book eliminates the earlier poem, "Envoy," which ended *Welcome Eumenides* self-dismissively by saying:

> better than any of you, poems,
> are the eyes
> that scribble themselves
>   across the sky
>   out the window
>   before dinner just as the doorbell rings
>   across the ceiling touched by carlights
>   at night when there are too many people to wake

Days Going / Days Coming Back has the same sense of an older stellar vision outweighing those crowds of nightsleepers, and any rival production of theirs in language. But as Taylor muses more openly about human abidance in relation to poetry, she begins to allow poetry a more durable function. "In the Bitter Roots" closes this impressive collection with a final image of the poet standing at the window, earlier travelers still in mind:

> Only to stand watching
> the chimneys take the sun,
> no sponge dry enough for the tears,
> no bowl adequate for the mixed feelings,
> only — she standing at the window
> by the gulf
> trapped in these mountains
> trapped in this face,
> bewildering decay,
> like him without one prayer,
> one begging phrase
> blown toward Virginia and native gods.

This woman standing at the window, thinking about Clark's expedition and Jefferson's legacies, and finding definition for her own, nonetheless has never relinquished a jot of the individuality which has always marked her work. It's interesting, too, to see that while history deeply informs everything she's written, Taylor's love of history does not extend to the side-branch, literary history, or her place in it. While there is a birth date for the poet, 1920, no publication dates appear on any page of this new book for her previous ones, the first of which, when I do a little burrowing elsewhere, shows itself to have been written when she was forty. Nor is there a shred of biography. It is very clear that she has reached a stage in which she wishes to be represented as a poet by her poems alone. The last lines of *Days Going/ Days Coming Back* conclude, not entirely with anonymity, or without self-reflection:

> Can I think to find
> a past, a past self, in these passes,
> in hospital at Sevastapol,
> following among Comanche squaws?
> Yes, and more,
> I proceed without a guide
> at this stage of the expedition
> though it's known madness.

Maybe it's a piece of luck not to have gotten beyond Clark's stupendous mountains, and like a female Antaeus to be rooted to what not only makes you at times bitterly and silently anarchic, but also seasons whatever you swallow with your own stubbornly original and distinctive wisdom.

Eleanor Ross Taylor: An Appreciation

The voice of Eleanor Ross Taylor's poetry is unmistakable. Colloquial without being folksy, literary without being high-handed, always innovative in their use of language ("unthought-up," "shutterflux," and "skytramping" are among her invented words), her poems are, above all, compelling to read. If one agrees with Donald Justice that "it remains the first duty of the poet to be *interesting*," then Taylor's poems are among the most fully realized in the last fifty years of American poetry. Their subjects—which range from the sixteenth-century Spanish conquest of Florida to a woman's meditations on a yellow jacket caught in her taxi—are as various as their modes, which include first-person lyrics, longer poems, and dramatic monologues. In addition, Taylor is a master of many different techniques: her metrics are as finely tuned as Frost's, and her free verse is as wide open and searching as Charles Olson's, while eschewing consciously avant-garde pyrotechnics. Randall Jarrell was right, forty years ago, to claim that these poems could "be good almost as Dickinson's or Hardy's poems are" (although in light of her most recent work it seems appropriate to jettison "almost"). Like Hardy, Taylor explores the possibilities of the dramatic mono-logue, and of narration within essentially lyric poems; she also shares his preoccupations with elegy and intergenerational fam-ily history—often, in Taylor, the latter two are very much re-lated. With Dickinson, Taylor shares a fascination for the kind of introspection that can only arise from a condition of extreme solitude ("Always Reclusive," one recent poem is aptly titled); and the music of her poems is often as startlingly individual as Dickinson's.

The importance of region in Taylor's work simply cannot be overstated. These poems are grounded in the consciousness of a woman whose familiarity with Southern history, culture, and landscape is profound. One of her primary subjects is the way in which wilderness—psychic and geographical—is both contained by domesticity and constantly threatening to overtake it. This tension has everything to do with the history of white women in the male-dominated, white supremacist South; and it is embodied in the music and rhythms of the poems, wherein a restrained, almost genteel tone is shot through with "a passion always threatening to go undisciplined with the characteristic intensity of her native South" (in the apt wording of *Days Going / Days Coming Back*'s jacket copy). Many of her best poems are portraits of Southern women; one of my favorites in this vein is "Epitaph," whose two middle stanzas read:

> Her house was screenless; doors stood wide;
> Leaves drifted unwatched down the hall;
> Hens left warm eggs indoors.
> A stray lamb maddened by the scolding floor
> Galloping broom to bed to wall to wall
> Fell out the back door finally, prayers-answered.
>
> For she was always in the low-grounds
> Chopping cotton, or by the orchard
> Binding wheat with wheat-strands,
> Thinning the corn slips in the new-ground field,
> Then home to snatch the coffee pot
> Up off the floor (where the baby'd played),
> Lay table, before they all got in.

This passage combines the breadth and specificity of great fiction with the intimacy of a lyric poem in a way that is uniquely Taylor's. The details of rural life are precisely and lovingly evoked — who wouldn't be drawn to this "stray lamb's" dilemma, made all the more visceral by the wholly original combination of "scolding floor," and the Taylorian grammatical hybrid, "prayers-answered" — in the service of the poem's elegiac purpose. The difficulty of the subject's life, consumed in farm- and housework, is not shirked or idealized; yet the poem's aim is not the portrayal of hardship, but the distillation of character — an aim which is brilliantly fulfilled in its concluding stanza:

> —Kate, this brew's not fit to drink.
> —What? . . .
>   Oh Lord.

> — Don't cry, Kate
> — But I can't help it.
> I never cried for shirtwaists
> Or China cups
> Or crocheted pillow shams. I've not.
> But oh to have it said of me
> She boiled the gosling in the coffee pot. . . .
> Poor gosling!

Such an abrupt switch from third-person description to dialogue is characteristic of Taylor, who makes this kind of Modernist strategy wholly her own throughout her work. What could better illuminate "Kate's" brand of backwoods forthrightness and integrity than her own mournful self-appraisal: "Poor gosling!"? The colloquial poignancy evident in this exchange is a fitting counterpoint to the preceding descriptive passage. Only a poet of rare genius could infuse this anecdote—bluntly homespun without becoming hokey—with such unassuming dignity. (It would be wrong to leave "Epitaph" without a nod to its accomplished and subtle metric. Taylor weaves back and forth between iambic dimeter and pentameter, even in the spoken section, both casually and masterfully in a way that recalls her contemporaries, Bishop and Lowell.)

More recently, Taylor's poems have shifted from a rural to a predominantly suburban Southern milieu. In "Retired Pilot Watches Plane," the speaker observes her suburban neighbor on an early morning dog-walk "stopped/midstreet looking up/The early NY flight/slowing for coming in":

> His head
> turning with the plane   a maze
> of speeds and altitudes?
> controls he is unleashing
> there in the cockpit?
> Half dizzy
> I come down to
> my yard   yews my late
> husband planted   East and color
> raying far   no line between
> earth's atmosphere
> black space   no oxygen

Taylor's use of stepped tercets, spacing, and spare punctuation in these lines helps to reinforce a sense of the vastness, both terrifying and exhilarating, not just of the open sky but of outer space, making its presence felt in this sedate neighborhood. And since early on the poem's speaker admits to the speculative nature of her ruminations ("He sees?   I can't know   More/than my party-talk/acquaintance wouldn't help"), we are fully aware that the true subject here is not the retiree's memory of flight but the speaker's imagination of that memory: "Half dizzy," *she* is the one who "come[s] down to/[her] yard." Down from where? From a place, I would speculate, that is halfway between the pilot's imagined cockpit, and the speaker's own inner experience of "a maze/of speeds and altitudes," of psychic "controls . . . unleash[ed]." The poem ends on a characteristically wry note — "I think I'll wait a minute/to get my paper in" — that both belies and reinforces the seriousness of its introspection: although the intent observation of her neighbor ("as/through a telescope") has prompted this potent confrontation with amplitude, the speaker knows a face-to-face greeting would betray that encounter's essentially private nature.

In the stanza quoted above, "raying" is a small but significant example of Taylor's word-play, which manages to combine Southern vernacular speech with a sophisticated, and specifically literary awareness of the possibilities of word usage — her vocabulary is as quirky and voluminous as Stevens's. The preceding may be an inept characterization, however, because I don't think Taylor is really opposing the vernacular to literary sophistication; rather, she has created a hybrid of the two all her own, as in the opening lines from "Shaking the Plum Tree":

Such light there was.
Ben up the plum tree,
    red plums snaked with light,
gold veins jagging in the plum skins
    like metal boiling,
plums bolting, knocking, to the ground,
    the sky, a huge shade-tree of light
tenting the stubblefield with centigrade. . . .

I'm struck by how this passage manages so seamlessly to juxta-
pose language that sounds spoken—the first line, and "Ben up
the plum tree" (where's the verb?)—with wildly inventive words
like "snaked" and "jagging"; there is, as well, an echo of Keats in
"stubblefield," and finally, the introduction of scientific diction
with "centigrade." To pack these different, almost divergent,
kinds of word-usage and association together in a poem that
manages to sound utterly natural is quite a feat, and one Taylor
pulls off over and over.

A poem in her first book, *Wilderness of Ladies*, is entitled
"Woman as Artist," and much of Taylor's work has addressed
the difficulty of balancing a domestic identity (daughter, wife,
mother) with an artistic identity; her more recent work looks at
this question from the perspective of a woman in her sixties and
seventies. In "Converse," she writes, "The artist has two
guises/in one time/and so must I." I take these "two guises" to
be the domestic self, participating in life, and more specifically in
family relationships, countered by the artistic or introspective
self, which flourishes most in solitude, both observing and imag-
ining the former self's life. The juxtaposition—and, at times, opposition—of these two related selves or "guises" fuels a great
many of Taylor's poems, including "Cuts Buttons Off an Old
Sweater," which contrasts a woman's purposeful daytime activity—"It takes a dark, thin book to tray the pickings/(they're
hard to gather off her skirt, the floor)/and chute them in the
trash can . . ./And it takes time. Minutes she crooked from the
hour,/shoplifted from the day"—with her dream life—"The
dream was . . ./crashing tall ironweed,/hushed, purple fire-
works/whispering fragrance/and light years of taking leave . . ."
The time spent dreaming, reckless and incautious, is character-
ized as "an hour of some real use," as contrasted with housework's "devised delay"; yet I find that the language in the
poem's first section, with its precision and genuine interest in the
subject's labor, her search for "such buttons, flat, dime-
sized,/that might be useful on another sweater,/a weary blouse,
some baby shirt," to be much more vital and interesting than
that in the dream section. This considerably complicates the
poem's appraisal of activity undertaken under the "guise" of

domesticity, and maybe that's the point. In "Long-Dreaded Event Takes Place," we find the speaker's self split in two under much more dire conditions, namely the illness and death of a loved one. Here, the distancing "guise" is more specifically that of an artist: "it blurs/happening as on a canvas/distanced . . . / as I/remote, half turned away,/my eyes half closed/half watch,//a painter   at my easel/distancing my sketch/pretending I recede. . . . " It's notable that Taylor chooses to portray grief's numbing effect in terms of artistry: even under the pressure of such a terrible event the fundamental sense of a bifurcated identity remains intact—and is perhaps even heightened.

"Long-Dreaded Event Takes Place" can be presumed to address—however obliquely—the death of the poet's husband, novelist Peter Taylor. Readers who approach her latest book, *Late Leisure*, expecting to find poems that confront this material head-on, as in Hardy's "Poems of 1912-13" or, more recently, the elegies of Tess Gallagher and Ruth Stone, may be frustrated by Taylor's reticence, so seemingly outmoded in our age of disclosure. But it is the tension between privacy and revelation that invigorates Taylor's work and produces some of her most vivid writing, as in "Long-Dreaded Event Takes Place":

> glazed eyes catching
> small smithereens:
> the nurse's ring
> bone pink smooth though modified
> the brief convulsive reflex
> and the driver's shoes well tied
> . . . . .
> later somewhere
> I'll paint-in gaps, fill in
> the larger picture,
> withholdings spilled
> out of my pockets of resistance—

What makes Taylor's poems uniquely compelling is the extent to which "the larger picture" is so often *not* "fill[ed] in"; and while the accumulation of these chilling "smithereens" is related to this poem's attempt to enact a grief-stricken consciousness, it seems to me that her work as a whole presents the reader with scraps

of consciousness and perception that it is our job to render co-
herent. From Eliot onward, this kind of aesthetic has been familiar to poetry readers; what makes Taylor's application of it so
inventive is the extent to which her method seems so much a
piece of her own particular personality and consciousness. The
terms in which Jarrell states this are enduring and useful: "The
poems are full of personal force, personal truth—the first and
last thing a reader sees in a writer—down to the last piece of
wording. Their originality is so entire, yet so entirely natural,
that it seems something their writer deserves no credit for: she
could do no other. . . . [T]hey are so much the direct expression
of the object that their words are still shaking with it—are, so to
speak, *res gestae*, words that, repeated, are not hearsay evidence
but part of the fact itself." This characterization of her work
holds true as much for her latest book as for her first, in which
the taste of life, both experienced and meditated on, is as present—almost—as a living person.

Finally, Taylor's meditations on the mystery of existence (for
lack of a less corny phrase) are what draw me most to her work.
"Infinity runs in your veins," she writes in "Mother's Blessing";
and in her poems an awareness of infinity within temporal and
corporeal existence is imbued with both wonder and fear. "Casting About," a recent long poem about—what else?—fishing, contains this emblematic passage:

> This new alluring world's still not my own.
> I go into its darkness
> as if I'm speeding on a train at night,
> my berth shade raised,
> and strange lights crashing by—
> racing into secrets on ahead,
> secrets fleeting, unaware I'm glimpsing them—
> my own solution, like one's palm,
> unfathomable to oneself.

Is it too crafty to read "berth" as a pun on *birth*? It seems to me
that the speaker of these lines is both a child about to be born
and an aged person on the verge of death, whose awareness of
his or her own "unfathom[ability]" is both "alluring" and
"strange." In this liminal realm, even the enigma of identity car-

ried by the speaker possesses its own subjectivity: "secrets . . . unaware I'm glimpsing them." The frisson of existential trepidation, so viscerally present in these lines, is equally apparent in "Hatchways," an eerie lyric whose speaker ponders the possible source of a nightmare ("Sleeping rapidly/I climb desperately/a hatchway mercilessly/narrow-channeled"):

> is that
> soon-to-be-born
> blood of my blood,
> two hundred miles away,
> gathering his-or-her strength
> (mixed with mine)
> on the private, drowsy
> sea of amnion,
> something like thought
> disturbing its red cobweb:
>   *No choice now*
>   *Only the job that all flesh must —*
> he-or-she summoning
> our strength for being hurled
> through the dread channel to
> the raw bite of the world?

Taylor's brilliance is nowhere more apparent than in this evocation of gestation and birth as an emblem of human experience's threat, possibility—and inscrutability. Her poems manage to combine the specificities of cultural and historic experience with archetypal, subterranean knowledge—"something like thought," but more deeply and uncannily sensed than thought: an insight both fearful and necessary, which one is reduced to stammering in the attempt to elucidate. Having looked at two passages that evoke birth and death more or less metaphorically, I'd like to conclude with an excerpt from "Maternity Ward," which juxtaposes its title's setting with a hospital's top floor "where men push muffled mops/not to wake ears from dying." These final lines' unnerving epiphany will, I hope, compel readers to range back through the unexpected, idiosyncratic, and always rewarding pleasures of Eleanor Ross Taylor's poems:

Vapors and shadows flicker: thin,
    terminal grandfathers vaporizing;
    new nebulae gathering, slowly,
    a maze of motes.
A nurse dreams through her graveyard-shift schedule
    in this time-marriage. Our flesh
    delivers ghosts.

Eleanor Ross Taylor and Silence

My son is nearly three years old and not yet embarrassed by his inconsistencies. He seems enraptured by the movie *The Jungle Book*, for instance, but as he sat watching it late one afternoon— while I, sitting opposite on the couch, used the temporary calm to grade papers and decipher memos—I noticed a shadow rise behind his eyes, a strange look for such a little boy to manage. Nothing much seemed to be happening in the movie: Mowgli, the wolf-boy, had decided to make a go of it on his own, feeling betrayed by his big, blustery buddy, Baloo the bear, who had just announced that Mowgli must return to the Man-Village. Mowgli was clambering over rocks beside a stream, crying softly, throwing rocks into the water. Having seen the movie a few dozen times, I knew that soon he would arrive in the waste-land just beyond the fringe of the jungle, where four vultures with cockney accents (and curiously resembling the Beatles) would befriend him. At that point the movie rushes quickly to its rather adult conclusion: boy is saved from the jaws of Shere Khan, the evil tiger, by friend (Baloo); boy in turn saves friend from same jaws; boy then, in the quiet aftermath of battle, sees girl (his first human); boy desires girl; boy loses desire to stay in jungle with friend he's just saved; boy wanders off after girl to live happily ever after in the Man-Village, leaving behind his understanding animal friends. The fairy tale ending is qualified by the suggestion (articulated by Baloo) that things will probably now get complicated for Mowgli, that a bear's life (eating ants and bananas and lounging around on the sun-warmed stones) has become the path not taken. Alas.

Naturally, as a reluctant academic, I was thinking the above thoughts as the movie unspooled, mentally writing my response to an ending that was still a few minutes off. But my son had stopped watching his favorite movie. He leaned forward and slipped from the chair, walked into the dining room and stood staring into the kitchen, where there was no one and nothing to stare at. He stood there for nearly a minute, until I rose and went to see what he was looking at. Nothing. "What is it, Walt?" I asked. He looked up at me, the shadow still present behind his eyes. "I don't like the tiger," he said. At that moment, in the next room, a roar emerged from the television as Shere Khan pounced on the helpless wolf-boy. I realized that Walt had also been thinking a few minutes ahead into the movie, and that he was now looking, quite purposefully, at nothing; that is, he was choosing not to look at what he knew was there, opting instead for the nothing that is, a nothing so loaded with his fears and few memories, with his inchoate imaginings of order transposed into the movie playing on the TV and in his mind, that he had been rendered speechless and nailed to the floor of that dining room by the tiger he expected to appear at any second in the kitchen. Life's like that for kids, and I sort of remembered feeling the same way once.

So much for Disney. I picked up Walt and carried him back to the living room, where we watched Mowgli attach a burning branch to the tiger's tail, watched the tiger run toward the horizon of the wasteland chased forever by fire, watched our hero return to the home he never knew he had, watched him resolve a separation he never knew existed. Walt summed it up nicely: "I don't like that tiger." Me neither. Then he asked if we could watch *The Jungle Book* again.

I thought of this little scene the morning after teaching a graduate seminar in which six smart and talented students of poetry and I sat in silence with a recent poem by Eleanor Ross Taylor, "Night Retrieves," from her remarkable new book *Late Leisure*. It could have been any poem from the book, any poem from her rich oeuvre, a body of work so startling and elusive that it incites that most vivid of silences: the group of devoted poets, heads bent, a sort of prayer taking place, a recognition occurring of poetry's most important tasks, those things not usurped by newer media and their hurried and effective means: the simple enactment of complicated contradictions; the ineffable given language; a representation of the simultaneity of experience (the nexus of the present brought to life, swollen to bursting by the past, by small traces of the future—usually the lingering fragrance of hope, a few of its feathers); the present presented as a painful irony: a life filled with ghosts.

Like so many of Taylor's poems, especially the recent ones, the poem begins *in medias res* in more ways than one: we're dropped into the middle of an ongoing dramatic situation, into the stream of an engaged consciousness, into the midst of a sentence or phrase or some other less defined linguistic unit:

> Smoking forest and red bees
> snapped-off at zenith
>   don't care for
>   morning, nor
> my yard's plaited trees.
>
> I was looking for holly? With Benedict?

It's difficult to get your feet under you in these lines. For instance, is it the speaker or the forest who doesn't care for morning, and by extension for the plaited trees? And why the questions? Shouldn't the speaker know what she was doing and with whom? But that's part of the point with Taylor. Over the years she has become a master of the blurred instant, of representing a moment in time that is literally overflowing with present-tense sensation, memory, description and figuration. What she does so well is mingle all of these, so that the typical dynamic of her poetry is an oddly (and paradoxically) static movement: spatial and temporal shifts, literal and metaphorical dissolves. We remain fixed in time, doomed by time, but somehow impervious to its linear requirements. It's easy to see why one of my students was literally shaken by the compression of this poem, by its evocation of the haunting power of loss, how it transforms the lived moment into something both less and more intensely perceived. Again, the contradictions are central to Taylor's poetry, just as they are to my son's sense of reality. His of course are a result of inexperience; hers of nearly too much experience. The poem proceeds through a brief evocation of the dramatic action ("He'd [Benedict] just called back,/'Here's some!' I, hurrying to/the sought-for ache") and an even slighter snippet of memory ("streets of St. Augustine/laid in Gambier, time-quaked"). The penultimate gesture is an intense meditation on a spider that has suddenly loomed into frame and which quickly becomes a figure for the parceling out of time (the steady spinning of her web). The poem ends with a line quoted from the dramatic moment, "*Where, Benedict?*" It's a truly startling poem whose proximity to consciousness is perilously close, and whose representation of disorientation—a disorientation of time—is almost too vivid. Again and again in *Late Leisure* we are brought up against the slippery mechanics of time, as if the easy progression of moments has been disrupted by the palpable presence of death. It's scary stuff, but thrilling, too, and utterly intoxicating.

I can remember quite clearly reading Eleanor Ross Taylor for the first time, and I will admit straight away that I came to her work late. She is what some critics call a poet's poet, which in this case means a neglected poet, though even that term is loaded with inappropriate suggestions. Taylor has always had a devoted following, a not insignificant band of loyalists (Randall Jarrell was once among them) who regularly champion her in the poetry press, spread the word with xeroxes of her recent work, a poem in *The Kenyon Review*, another in *The Southern Review*, the monumental few that shook the tight margins of *The New Yorker* with their vivid strangeness. All of this is a way to say that I'd simply not talked to the right people, not opened the right pages at the right time. Reading is like that sometimes: a chain of accidents that occasionally adds up to a recognition of brilliance, but more often results in a now-and-then encounter with the lovely and memorable. So it wasn't until the early 90s that I finally picked up a collection of hers, the compendium (how else to describe it?) titled *Days Going / Days Coming Back*. And the poem I opened to was "Short Foray."

The poem is both typical for Taylor and rather aberrant, typical in its concentrated focus, its lyric pressure on a single instant, aberrant in its dramatic clarity, its paraphrasability. The speaker is in a taxi on her way, presumably, to deliver a recently purchased gift to her one-year-old grandchild, when a yellow jacket flies in the car and initiates a meditation on response; that is, a consideration of the difference in her response and the taxi driver's. We learn that the speaker is allergic to bees, that her age and health make this threat all the more poignant, and that she has now lost what she had been thinking about just prior to the yellow jacket's entrance: her inability to remember what a one-year-old would like as a gift, a two-fold loss of the past since she cannot, naturally, remember her own infancy, but also cannot remember her child's. This isn't so great a concern, perhaps, but in a manner typical of Taylor she very quickly ups the ante. After considering briefly the thoughts of the taxi driver, whose life is completely unavailable to her outside the realm of imagination, she returns her attention to the yellow jacket, which has exited the taxi and alighted on another vehicle in traffic:

> When we moved on I lost the yellow jacket,
>   lost whether he kept clinging to the truck,
>   went to the bank, or soared off over us.
> No clue to what he meant, rushing my taxi.
> Did he know it was October, bees-up time,
>   and take this warm day for a last rich look
>   at the boundaries of things, a day of
>   stinging a boundary or two if he felt like it,
>   playing time bomb?
> Did he smell wild asters somewhere in a ditch?
> Or did he just ride into town on that pickup
>   and mean to go home on it?

That last line is one of the few traces of southern vernacular in Taylor's work; she tends to parcel out accents, choose words and fashion phrases with the precision of a jewel cutter; her poems are the glittering accumulation of many tiny choices, and they are understood best holistically rather than through a continuous parsing of individual pieces. A phrase like "stinging a boundary," for instance, is characteristic of Taylor, a subtle example of linguistic complication; by extending the connotative suggestions of the word boundary, she heightens in a dazzling way the very image of the body sitting in the taxi, its skin a literal and figurative armor. And of course, mortality is the subject, wonderfully complicated by its ironic symbiosis in this case, since when a bee stings someone allergic to bees, both will drag themselves off to die. The last line suddenly takes on more meaning, becomes more than a small joke, a throw away. It is emblematic of Taylor, a poet who never writes for long without considering the absolute privilege of making art, who can never help but see such a privilege as luxury, and who time and time again pokes sly fun at the activity of rendering the things of the world symbolic and figuratively significant. This relationship to the activity of art probably has something to do with her age and gender, with the fact of her role as wife and mother for so many years, how the demands of her life often required the sacrifice of her art (Adrienne Rich has addressed this issue more than once in the context of Taylor's poems). Out of necessity, Taylor writes reflexively about the workings of consciousness in an individual moment, and does so more successfully than almost any poet of her generation (Ashbery is an oddly comparable poet in this re- gard, though who would think of him when reading Taylor?). But the manner of this reflexive writing feels so earned, so much a product of circumstance; her poems feel lifted from ordinary moments and are charged with extraordinary meditative juxta- positions, as if their speakers were saying, "These moments have been my province for so long that I've come to recognize their fullness, their synecdochical significance in the contemplation of the eternal."

To go back to my originating anecdote, Eleanor Ross Taylor has considered the nothing that is for so long that she is able to bring enormous gravity to very simple, often domestic moments. My son looked away from the present, knowing what the future would bring, and stood staring at a nothing, appreciating its si- lence, feeling every sensation of the present, even as his memo- ries of the movie mingled with his anticipation of what was about to happen in it, a strange coincidence of past and future. What's important to note is how small my son's present moment is compared to Taylor's, who brings to each instant under scru- tiny a choir of ghosts, a host of dreams and countless reels of filmed memory. One never knows in these poems what will ap- pear and why, because they are perfect representations of the ac- cident of the present, the collision of the past (most often what has been lost), with a foreshortened future, all of it played out in a context of immediacy, of intense sensation. And of course, it is a foreshortened future for all of us, since we see quite clearly where the lines lead, how briefly they inscribe the landscape, how they lead to nothing, a vanishing point on the horizon.

I used the quote from Stevens ("the nothing that is") deliberately, since Taylor's project is not so different. If Stevens married existential concerns to virtuosic verbal music (trusting that meaning would take care of itself), then Taylor has left the music out of the mix, preferring instead to allow the existential uncertainties to float to the jagged surfaces of her often severely fractured poems. Which isn't to say that beauty has gone missing. There's a feminist poetics at work in these lines, a nearly Sapphic trust in disruption, hesitation and silence (to paraphrase Louise Gluck). I heard William Matthews say once that poetry is the silence around which we orchestrate sound. The suggestion there is that it's the silence we're most interested in, a silence that begets beauty. Stevens again.

Richard Howard

Foreword to *Welcome Eumenides*

"After you I go, my life! Was it chase or flight?"

In Castalia, not far from where I was raised in northeast Ohio, there is a place called The Blue Hole, which I used to be taken to see as a child: it is a small pond, apparently without source or outlet, blue indeed and said to be bottomless—there is the inevitable story of the team of horses accidentally driven into it one winter night a century ago and never found, though grappled for at unimaginable depths. The Blue Hole is a mysterious site, nor can its mystery be vulgarized, even in northeast Ohio where windshield souvenirs attest your visitation, for there is a silence about this body of water (the expression seems only justice, for once), an unexpected presence from below that keeps the gum-wrappers from polluting such fountains with which poetry has always been associated, as the name Castalia itself reminds us. Of course The Blue Hole is not really bottomless, merely the sudden surfacing, among trivial mediations, of an underground river which then vanishes once more; the team of horses cannot be dragged to the surface because it has been carried away, perhaps the skeletons, or, who knows—say the water is a marinade and the team entire, rolling eyes, streaming manes and tails—will reappear the next time this subterranean source remounts, abstergent, unplumbed, clear, giving back whatever it took into itself.

This natural miracle is before us—it has occurred in the work of Eleanor Ross Taylor. A dozen years ago her first book of poems, *Wilderness of Ladies,* was published with a brilliant introduction by Randall Jarrell "to make it easier for the readers to consider the possibility of the poems' being what they are"; what they are, as our great poet-critic exulted, is a world, like Hardy's or Janacek's, "the water/meeting me around the curve . . . the waiting womb! the waiting tomb—/the empty antique sitting room!"—precisely, birth, life, and the process that divides and unites them. Now, after long silence, we are given that speech again, "etched with inheritance and fate," eager yet reticent, reckless and still patient, solicitous, attentive, nursing (it is capital that one of the major pieces here is a dramatic reverie uttered by Florence Nightingale, a poem which gives the book its startling title).

I think Jarrell's prose did make it easier for readers, but perhaps it became harder for the poet, after such praise, such precision ("the world is a cage for a woman, and inside it the woman is her own cage . . . life is a state of siege, a war to the last woman"), to surface again, to welcome the Eumenides which are, we must remember, not the Erinyes, the Furies, but the Kindly Ones, mediators of ritual, functionaries of acceptance.

This new book of Mrs. Taylor's is our fortunate particular and proof that what had seemed a singular welling-up, an exceptional outpouring, is more for being carried on, for returning to observable earth, not just The Blue Hole but a longer look at what Matthew Arnold calls "the unregarded river of our life." We have watched, or at least we have waited, for that American talent which would seal the pact between Emily Dickinson and Walt Whitman, between that private extremity which is a crying need and that public extremity which is an inward wound. And here, with this second collection which includes "A Few Days in the South," the best poem since Whitman about the War Between the States, here is that talent, that reconciliation ("fever, flesh, ash into ashes burn") which is of course a new aggression, a new demand. It is a demand upon the poet herself, an insistence that she come to terms with her resources, with her impoverishment, and it reminds us that Eleanor Ross Taylor is the wife of Peter Taylor, one of our finest narrative writers to concern himself with the voice of a region, the vision of a class, the vaunt of a generation. It is a great thing for a poet to be married to a great prose writer, for his achievement shows her what she must keep overcoming in order to become what she is: a diction out of the shadows which does not erase itself as it is raised. Whereas the prose voice rubs itself out as it goes along, *her* voice must be somehow suspended, held up on its rhythms, its intervals, its silences, until no message is left but a resonance, no communication but an echo: persistent, yielding, heard.

Lest I, too, seem to outspeak Mrs. Taylor who is quite likely to sink back into her garden ("earth to earth, inside you yet/in the garden to come"), the buried stream proceeding to its next unpolicied embodiment, I would not claim for her more than her own purpose, so aptly asserted by her title. *Welcome Eumenides* (the diary notation of Florence Nightingale) is a rehearsal of what Jane Harrison means, in her famous chapter of the *Prolegomena*, "The Making of a Goddess," when she describes the growth of a function from imprecation and warding-off to acceptance and nourishment (nursing!) to welcoming and prayer. That is why the word *attendance* holds both the word for shelter and the word for tension within its etymon, and why, magnificently, Eleanor Ross Taylor will say—it is the way to read her, to let her reveal herself—

Our language exists but in silence,
Our mortality in immortality.

Introduction to *Wilderness of Ladies*

Buck Duke says to Mamma, as he brings her the milk-pail full of wild plums:

"Sour! Your eyes'll water, Miss Tempe!
But sweet, too."

The taste of someone else's life—and while you are reading the poems of Eleanor Taylor you are someone else—is almost too sour to be borne; but sweet, too. The life is that of one woman, one (as the census would say) housewife; but a family and section and century are part of it, so that the poems have the "weight and power,/Power growing under weight" of a world. Some of this world is grotesquely and matter-of-factly funny, some of it is tragic or insanely awful—unbearable, one would say, except that it is being borne. But all of it is *so*, seen as no one else could see it, told as no one else could tell it.

The poems and poet come out of the Puritan South. This Scotch Presbyterianism translated into the wilderness is, for her, only the fierce shell of its old self, but it is as forbidding and compulsive as ever: the spirit still makes its unforgiving demands on a flesh that is already too weak to have much chance in the struggle. The things of this world are "what Ma called poison lilies, sprouting/From Back Bunn's meadow resurrection-wise/But with a sinful pink stain at the throat." So much, still, is sin! Blaming the declining West, a character in one of the poems says hotly: "You talk so much of rights, now;/You ask so seldom what your duties are!" The poet knows too well for asking what her duties are, and has no rights except the right to do right and resent it: her "Lord, help me to be more humble in this world!" is followed without a pause by the exultant "In that Great, Getting-up Morning, there will be another song!" She cannot permit herself—the whole life she has inherited will not permit her—to be happy, innocently bad, free of these endless demands, this continual self-condemnation. Frost speaks of a world where work is "play for mortal stakes," but here everything is work for mortal stakes, and harder because of the memory of play, now that nothing is play. (I once heard a woman say about buying new clothes for a trip to Europe: "It's work, Mary, it's work!" —a very Protestant and very ethical sentence.)

First there were her own family's demands on the girl, and now there are the second family's demands on the woman; and worst of all, hardest of all, are the woman's demands on herself—so that sometimes she longs to be able to return to the demands of the first family, when the immediate world was at least childish and natural, and one still had child allies in the war against the grown-ups. Now the family inside—the conscience, the superego—is a separate, condemning self from which there is no escape except in suicide or fantasies of suicide, the dark rushing not-I into which the I vanishes. And which, really, is the I? The demanding conscience, or the part that tries to meet— tries, even, to escape from—its demands? In one poem the chain gang guard envies the prisoner who still needs a guard, who cannot escape because of the rifle outside, the guard outside; the guard himself no longer has to be guarded, says in despairing mockery: "Here I stand! loaded gun across me—/As if I'd get away!" The world is a cage for women, and inside it the woman is her own cage. In longing regression, this divided self—"riding the trolley homeward this afternoon/With the errands in my lap"—would willingly have let it all slide from her lap, would willingly have "disfestooned my world—/A husband, more or less!/A family, more or less!/To have alighted to a cup of kettle-tea/And someone/To whom I could lie merrily,/Use malapropisms, be out-of-taste"; to the sister who is "more than one-flesh-and-blood,/Almost one I." The self, two now, longs for that first world in which it and another were, almost, one; longs to return to the make-believe tea that preceded the real tea of the grown-ups, the tea that, drunk, makes one a wife and mother.

The world of the poems is as dualistic as that of Freud; everything splits, necessarily, into two warring opposites. This fault along which life divides, along which the earthquakes of existence occur, is for the poet primal. It underlies all the gaps, disparities, cleavages, discontinuities that run right through her; she could say with Emerson: "There is a crack in everything that God has made." She says about her sister and herself: "The wars of marriage and the family burst around us"; but these are only external duplicates of the war inside, the war of self and self. Life is a state of siege, of desperate measures, forlorn hopes, last extremities—is war to the last woman. Carried far enough, everything reduces to a desperate absurdity; one can say about the poems themselves what one of the poems says about a man: "You were a mortal sheen/Flickering from the negative." The poems' Religious Wars, wars of conscience, go over into wars of anxiety and anguish, of neurosis or psychosis: "For me the expected step sinks,/The expected light winks/Out . . ." The water of sexuality, of unknown experience, that the child shrank from and that the woman longs to drown in, freezes into glass, gems, the hard "stock-dead" fixity of catatonia:

> Oh to have turned at the landing
> And never have sounded the bell
> That somehow thrust me into this room
> Beaded with eyes, painfully held
> To the liable frame I illume.
> Could life stop, or go on!
> But olives dangle crystal stems,
> And that clock muffles its French tick
> In those elaborate kiss-me-knots;
> Does it, too, hate its gems?

In frigid aberration, she spoils the life she ought to nourish: "Each year I dug and moved the peonies/Longing to flare/Fat and chemically by the well-slab,/Ingrown./Every day I opened the drawer and/Scanned the knives." And the warped spirit (after it has desperately demanded, from outside, the miracle that alone could save it: "You should have struck a light/In the dark I was, and/Said, Read, Be—be over!") ends in an awful negative apotheosis, as it cries: "Not in the day time, not in the dark time/Will my voice cut and my poison puff/My treasures of flesh,/My gems of flashing translucent spirit,/Nor my caress shatter them." When in another poem a patient says: "It nettled me to have them touch my dog/And say in their dispelling voices, *Dog*," the helpless, fretful, loving-its-own-psychosis voice of the psychotic is so human that your heart goes out to it, and can neither pigeonhole it nor explain it away. The violent emotion of so much of the poetry would be intolerable except for the calm matter-of-factness, the seriousness and plain truth, of so much else; and except for the fact that this despairing extremity is resisted by her, forced from her, instead of being exaggerated for effect, depended on as rhetoric, welcomed for its own sake, as it is in that existential, beatnik Grand Guignol that is endemic in our age. And, too, there is so much that is funny or touching, there are so many of the homely, natural beauties known only to someone "who used to notice such things." How much of the old America is alive in lines like "She took a galloping consumption/After she let the baby catch on fire . . . /And Cousin Mazeppa took laudanum./'Why did you do it, Zeppie girl?/Wa'n't Daddy good to you?'/'Pray, let me sleep!'"—Byron and Liszt and Modjeska end at this country crossroads, in a name. How could old-maidly, maiden-ladyish refinement be embodied more succinctly, funnily, and finally than in:

Miss Bine taught one to violet the wrists.
"I accuse you, Mr. Stapleton,
Of excess temperance—ha ha!"
"Miss Tempe . . . I beg. . . . Allow me to insist—!"

The old woman, dying among images, sees out on the dark river of death, past Cluster Rocks, "an old lady her uncles rowed across—/The boat beneath her slipped the bank/Just as she stepped ashore./'Stretched me arightsmart,' she chirped./O to think of that dying!/O unworthy 'Stretchedmearightsmart'!/She glared at hell through tears." This country humor, which comes out of a natural knowledge like that of Hardy or Faulkner, can change into a gallows-humor that once or twice has the exact sound and feel of Corbière: the suicide on her way into the water mutters, "It's no good God's whistling, 'Come back, Fido'"; the cold benighted lovers flee down the blocked-off "last bat-out-of-hell roads:/*Closed, Under Destruction*." But these and other humors—the humors of dreams, of neurosis, of prosaic actuality—

all come together in a kind of personal, reckless charm, an absolute individuality, that make one remember Goethe's "In every artist there is a germ of recklessness without which talent is inconceivable."

In the beginning there were no ladies in the wilderness, only squaws. These were replaced, some generations ago, by beings who once, in another life, were ladies; once were Europeans. To these lady-like women in the wilderness there is something precious and unnatural about lady-likeness, about the cultivated European rose grafted upon the wild American stem. But "pretense had always been their aim," even when in childhood they had played house, played grown-up. Their conscious female end is that genteel, cultured, feminist oldmaidishness that—intact, thorny, precisely self-contained—rises above the masculine, disreputable economic and sexual necessity that reaches out to strip off their blossoms, that makes you "dish potatoes up three times a day,/And put your wedding dress into a quilt," that turns young ladies into old women. This Victorian old-maidish culture has its continuation in the *House Beautiful, Vogue*-ish sophistication that the poet calls "Our exotic properties, our pretty price./The garden radish lies on ice, the radish rose./Smorgasbord!" The new *déjeuner sur l'herbe* is summed up, bitterly, in the old terms, the plain, religious, country terms: "Dinner on the grounds! and the blessing still unsaid. . . ." The poet looks askance at this acquired surface, even in herself—especially in herself, since it belongs neither to her wild heart nor to her neo-Calvinist conscience. To her there is something natural and endearing about the crushing wilderness, the homely childish beauties that one relaxes or regresses into. It is the ladies who really are barren, so that one might say: "You make a desert and call her a lady"; and in what is perhaps the most beautiful and touching of all these poems, "Buck Duke and Mamma," it is human feeling, natural sexuality, that the woman at last accepts in grief, and it is the histrionic feminine gentility that she rejects.

If these poems are less about the New Woman than about the Old (surviving, astonished, into this age of appliances and gracious fun), still, no poems can tell you better what it is like to be a woman; none come more naturally out of a woman's ordinary existence, take both their subjects and their images out of the daily and nightly texture of her life. Many of these are what I think of as woman's-work-is-never-done images: cooking, sewing, ironing, taking care of children, tending the sick, and so on; but these pass, by way of gardening, on over into the lady-like images of social existence, distrusted things akin to all the images of glass, mirrors, gems, of coldness, hardness, and dryness, of two-ness, cleavages, opposites, negatives, of trapped circular motion, that express a range of being from gentility to catatonia. These are lightened, colored, by images from childhood and the past—counting-out rhymes, hymns, slave songs, and so on. A pervading, obsessive image is that of light in darkness: there are so many stars, meteors, flames, snowflakes, feathers, that one almost feels that the poems themselves can be summed up in the sentence in which the dying old woman sums up her life: "My quick, half-lighted shower, are you gone?"

Often these last images merge with the ruling, final image of the poems, that of water: the water of experience or sexuality, into which the little girl is afraid to wade; the river the dying woman remembers from childhood and must cross, now, into the next world; life's dark star-bearing flood trapped in the mill of daily duties, of reduced mechanical existence: "The water pushes the mill wheel;/The wheel, wheeling, dispersing,/Disperses the starry spectacle/And drags the stone"—trapped, or else frozen into the fixity of glass, of mirrors, of the hateful gems that send the hands on in their aimless endless circle. Even sexual love is seen in terms of water freezing into—or melting among—the "thin floes," the cold clandestine darkness of a country night. You destroy yourself, escape from yourself, in water: in "Goodbye Family," "under the foundations of God's World/Lilily/Swimming on my side" until at last "the water/Meeting me around the curve, roaring, blanks/Out all"; and in "Escape," as "a vein of time gapes for her small transfusion," she or her double disappears into the ocean with a "far white crash, too negligible to bear." She says that "art and death" are "both oceans on my map"—the map of the "Woman as Artist," woman as lover. And woman ends, man ends, "lying at the edge of the water," face in the water: "when our faces are swol up/We will look strange to them./Nobody, looking out the door/Will think to call us in./They'll snap their fingers trying/To recollect our names"; the rope is broken, no one ever again will draw up the bucket bobbing at the bottom of the well of death. In the poems everything goes together, everything has several reasons for being what it is: the whole *Wilderness of Ladies* is, so to speak, one dream, that expresses with extraordinary fidelity and finality the life of the dreamer.

Many of the poems show (rather as the end of "The Old Wives' Tale" shows) what you might call human entropy—life's residual reality, what is so whatever else is so. That life, just lived, is death; that its first pure rapturous flame grows greater, fouls itself, diminishes, struggles and goes out: the poems say it with terrible magic:

> In the morning, early,
> Birds flew over the stable,
> The morning glories ringed the flapping corn
> With Saturn faces for the surly light
> And stars hung on the elder night.

But soon the sun is gone, the stars go out as the old woman's eyes close. Life is a short process soon over: how quickly the lyric, girlish, old-fashioned funniness of "My Grandmother's Virginhood, 1870" becomes the worn, sad grown-upness of "Motherhood, 1880"!—the girl's kiss so soon is the woman's sick or dying baby, her eroded featureless "They know I favor this least child."

The poems are full of personal force, personal truth—the first and last thing a reader sees in a writer—down to the least piece of wording. Their originality is so entire, yet so entirely natural, that it seems something their writer deserves no credit for: she could do no other. Just as the poems' content ranges from pure fact to pure imagination, so their language ranges from a folk speech as authentically delightful as Hardy's or Faulkner's (though the poet's use of folk material reminds me even more of Janacek's and Bartok's) to a poetic style so individual that you ask in wonder: How can anything be so queer and yet so matter-of-fact—natural, really? Picasso has said that when you find the thing yourself it is always ugly, the others after you can make it beautiful. Sometimes this is true of these poems; and yet sometimes she has found it beautiful, or has made it into a marvel you don't call either beautiful or ugly—have no words for:

> Was it forgiven? It was gone,
> The heathen dancing
> With her giggling sisters;
> They flew about the room
> In seedstitch weskits
> Like eight wax dolls gone flaskwards.
> Those were gay days!
> She sighed a mournful tune
> Waddling about her everyday
> Affairs of life and death
> (Affairs of painful life, uncertain death):
> "Wild loneliness that beats
> Its wings on life," she sang.
> She thwacked a pone in two,
> Her big hand for a knife.
> Thar! stirring it severely,
> And thar! into the oven. . . .

There is plenty of detached objective observation in the poems, but usually they are objective in another sense: they are so much the direct expression of the object that their words are still shaking with it—are, so to speak, *res gestae*, words that, repeated, are not hearsay evidence but part of the fact itself. The poet continually makes a kind of inevitable exclamation, has wrenched from her a law or aphorism, a summing-up, that is at the same time an animal cry. Sometimes her speech is the last speech before speechless desperation—too low to be heard as sound, only felt as pain; but sometimes it is like sunlight on fall leaves, firelight on cornbread. The book presents as they have never been presented before—which is to say, as every true artist has presented them—our everyday affairs of life and death.

Some of the very best of Eleanor Taylor's poems, I think, are "Buck Duke and Mamma," "Song," "Woman as Artist," "Moved," "Family Bible" (especially "Grandparents"), "The Bine Yadkin Rose," and "Goodbye Family"; poems like "Madame,"

"In the Churchyard," "The Chain Gang Guard," and "Playing" are slighter or smaller, but realized past change. Readers who are well acquainted with all of *Wilderness of Ladies* will feel an impatient disgust at me for some of the poems I haven't named, the qualities I haven't mentioned. And all the poems are far more than the best poems: the pieces, put together, are a world.

When one reads poems here and there, in magazines and manuscript—as I first read these—it seems very unlikely that they should be good almost as Dickinson's or Hardy's poems are. Of course the readers who first saw Dickinson's and Hardy's poems, in magazines and manuscripts, thought it just as unlikely that the poems should be good almost as Wordsworth's were. The readers knew what the poems weren't, what the poems couldn't be; and because of this it was hard for them to see what the poems were. An introduction to a book like *Wilderness of Ladies* might make it easier for readers to consider the possibility of the poems' being what they are.

Heather Ross Miller

Family Bible

Our writing class met in the Home Economics Building, its Greek Revival facade as heavy as Arlington, its gold letters flashing in the winter sun. Randall Jarrell called us "the little scorpions" because we were so quick to turn and sting each other. One afternoon he brought in a loose-page manuscript and began reading poems to us. I blinked, swallowed, sat up as the words stormed the room, the names of my family glowing and glowering among them: Whit Ross, Aminta Dunlap Watkins, Merina Wilkerson, Uncle Mun. And the family places: Cedar Grove, Rehobath. And the family images: honeycomb, anger, wild stars, death, innocent and secret joys, loneliness.

I thought for a minute I wrote the poems. But I knew these words were far too strong, accurate, resonant, and brilliant for me. I knew what they meant, I knew what they showed. But I could not have said a one of them, not yet.

Then Randall grinned straight at me, said, "These are from a new collection I'm writing an introduction for. And the poet is a graduate of Woman's College," and then I knew who she was, my Aunt Eleanor. The book _Wilderness of Ladies_, her first. Randall never said, _Oh, and by the way, Eleanor Ross Taylor is Heather's aunt._ He just grinned and kept on reading. He was testing me.

The little scorpions actually liked the poems, except for certain phrases using broad southern idiom, "If your Grandma aint thrown it out," "When our faces are swol up," "Stretched me arightsmart," and "Aint no curtain, aint no shade—/Don't hurt none to be afraid."

Randall was amused that her raw, down-to-nerves life offended them. He teased, "But don't you think the particular speaker, man or woman, would use exactly that kind of language?" They wrinkled freckled noses, shook heads, _No, poets don't do that._

They didn't trust the language the way she did.

And these are the hallmarks of her poems, anger, raw nerves, dangerous loyalty, bitter love, and trust, above all, trust. And family, not particularly heavenly or noble, but genuine, the real thing, richly blooded.

After class, Randall bubbled over to me, "Gee, from what all I know about genetics and heredity, this is really spooky. You and Eleanor sound just alike. The way you put things, the things that move you both." And he went on bubbling about her forthcoming book and her remarkable gifts, the same way he would bubble later, upon receiving the National Book Award, talking not of himself, but of the marvelous new poems of Eleanor Ross Taylor.

And that day in Greensboro, I was both proud and nervous and hotly envious. She sounded better than I did, put things stronger, sharper, and I had learned on the spot how a poem was supposed to work. And I was afraid I might not live up to her.

I always learned, on the spot, from her.

I had always tried to live up to her.

Listen to this:

Five years old, I'm visiting on a Sunday in my grandmother's house near Norwood, North Carolina, actually, a community known as Cedar Grove. A white-painted wooden Methodist Church down the dirt road rises on a mound of dark bristly cedars, so thick and fragrant, they spice the country air.

My Aunt Eleanor grew up in this house, probably about five years old herself when my grandparents built it and moved there. She has just introduced her new husband, my Uncle Peter Taylor, a blond man in an Army uniform, and then they drive away in a pale blue Ford V-8; the winter sun flashes so brightly it hurts me to look at it. The family calls me Heather Ann.

My grandmother sweeps the dining-room hearth with a broomstraw bundle, the soft swish of the fibers as comforting to me as the soft skin of her hands. She has little tears in the corners of her eyes. And I think I understand some of what is going on. My grandmother cries because she is happy for her daughter who just got married in Tennessee, but she is unhappy because her daughter's new husband is going overseas to World War II, somewhere in England. Overseas, that mysterious territory of exotic land and hard death.

And I watch all this when we say goodbye in the yard, in that brightly bitter sunlight. I love the dark blue velveteen bonnet tied under my chin, its stiff brim and little feather. The blue tweed coat and itchy leggings, I really hate, the little ankle zippers always come undone and bite into my skin. My laced-up leather shoes chalky with Griffin's polish give off a mildly acrid smell that mixes, I think, with the sunlight.

Then my aunt and her husband drive off in the Ford the shape and sheen of a blue Easter egg and we wave and hurry back inside to the dining-room fire where my grandmother takes up the broomstraw and begins sweeping, sweeping, pausing sometimes to study the hearth bricks.

Maybe, I think, this is how it is with aunts and grandmothers and new husbands and a war overseas. My Aunt Eleanor is very attractive, with smooth brown pageboy hair, rosy cheeks, and huge shy smiles. I like all this, yet it disturbs.

Such disturbance shows in her poems:

Typical of the presents
Grandma gave Grandpa
Was Uncle Mun,
A baroque buckle
Not to be undone.

The first poem in the sequence called "Family Bible," "Uncle" opens with a wry and clinical tone, its first word almost dismissive. The short choppy lines and the insistent rhythm, the alliterative image, "baroque buckle," that turns suddenly disturbing, if comic, "not to be undone," and features so prominently the first of a series of negatives, "not."

Grandma becomes "Grandmother," the second poem, continuing the disturbance and searching wistfulness of the sequence, seen, of course, from the point of view of a granddaughter. And life was too much and too hard:

She made her bed and it was hard, for rest
Too hard; when broken dreams and sleep encroached

Upon stark wakefulness, she walked the stars;
Her unread eye imagined what they meant:
Job's Coffin and the Seven Sisters, the fine-print
Groups.

The disappointments resonate: hard and stark and stars, wakefulness and walked and broken. More poems tell us this woman liked peacock feathers and dancing, cherry bounce and giggling. But now, after marriage to a good, though unrelenting man, a marriage with seven children and no frills:

"Wild loneliness that beats
Its wings on life," she sang.
She thwacked a pone in two,
Her big hand for a knife.
Thar! stirring it severely,
And thar! into the oven. . . .

There is a determination here, an insistence to see it through that I admire, not only in the poem, but also in the two women, the grandmother and the granddaughter who writes about her.

I packed my suitcase and ran away when I was five. The suitcase, made of black pasteboard, had a fake leatherette handle I especially liked, and fake gold clasps. I stuffed a bunch of junk in the suitcase and snapped it shut, pressing down the bulges. *There! There!* Nobody could tell me what to do.

And I set off down the red dirt road leading away from my grandmother's house and toward Badin, a small aluminum-smelting town seventeen miles north. My parents were in Badin, up to no good, I felt sure. I intended to burst into the apartment and show them they couldn't go off and leave me.

My Aunt Eleanor ran behind me, caught up and tried to get me to go back with her to the house. She told me about the things that would happen to me on the way to Badin. Kidnappers would get hold of me and chop me up in a hundred bloody pieces. They'd throw my arms in one place, my legs in another place. They'd send my head in a shoe box to my parents and get money.

I didn't care, kept on walking. Then she said, "Well, Heather Ann, if you're going, then I'm going with you."

I hadn't counted on that. She was more stubborn than I, and we both walked along, irritable and hot and put out with each other. I itched. I got thirsty, and I had to pee. My arm ached from the black suitcase and the fancy leatherette handle made a blister. My aunt stopped talking to me. She didn't even offer to carry the hateful suitcase.

An educated woman with the soul and energy of a poet, she already knew her mind. And I couldn't even read my name yet. She never gave up. She would dog my heels for the full seventeen miles. I had to figure a way out.

We reached the top of a small hill where four roads came together in a tumble of red dust and gravel: Macedonia, Norwood, Cottonville, Aquadale. I put down the suitcase, and a breeze sprang out of the woods and across the fields on either side of us. I loved the feel of it over my body, lifting my print skirt, making the hair on my sweaty head suddenly cool.

Aunt Eleanor waited patiently. She knew I had to fall back. And so I did. Turning around right there and walking back to my grandmother's house where I stormed inside and threw the suitcase against the wall.

"What's wrong with the baby?" asked my grandmother, turning from the stove full of simmering pots.

"Nothing." My aunt poured some iced tea, beat sugar up in the bottom of the glass. "Nothing at'all."

We never said another word about running away. About kidnappers. About bloody arms and legs and my head sent in a shoebox to my parents in Badin.

I think I glimpsed and, I hope, learned something of her persistence, her sense of responsibility, her maddening sort of family love.

For the granddaughter of the "Family Bible" has to speak out loud at last and show us her own kind of disturbance has been reconciled. She watches her grandmother, now "old, deaf, widowed," cross the yard of Rehobath Church with long black skirts and veils, her blue eyes roving the crowd:

> She seemed a giant Figure,
> All eyes upon her;
> Yet none spoke.

And all my heart said,
Run to her! Claim her!
(Wild loneliness that
Beats its wings on death)
Then the spell broke.
We who had waved across so many chasms
No longer had to say we were not close.
Was closeness more than painful separateness?
We were a constellation of detached, like, ghosts.

Reading the Poetry of Eleanor Ross Taylor

> Nature is a Haunted House—but
> Art—a House that tries to be
> haunted.

ଔ   ଔ   ଔ

> Tell all the Truth but tell it slant
>
> —Emily Dickinson

I'm walking in woods on a still, winter's day. I come to a pond that's iced-over, the surface smooth and polished as a lens. Not far from shore, an irregular shape made where someone or something fell through. The ice isn't thick and I wonder how someone could have misjudged the jeopardy of walking on it. I pause; there's no sound now but my heart beating and my breath.

The story of what happened here is not told by the body itself, but by the abstract shape of jagged ice lines that surround the place where the body broke through. How those lines are straight and strong as if cut along the crystal's grain by a keen blade; no swerving, no softening into sentimental curves. What those lines form is the story—a series of fierce slants and zigzags precisely circumferencing some significant truth that disappeared below a surface or moved on after a shattering experience.

Woman Observing, Preserving, Conspiring, Surviving: The Poems of Eleanor Ross Taylor

Eleanor Ross Taylor's first book, *Wilderness of Ladies*, published in 1960, recognized by a handful of people including the late Randall Jarrell, has remained an underground book, fierce, rich, and difficult, though it seems less "difficult" with every passing year, just as Emily Dickinson does. In that book are two poems I've carried about with me for a decade as a kind of secret knowledge and reinforcement: "Woman as Artist" and "Sister." They, like many of Eleanor Taylor's poems, speak of the underground life of women, the southern white Protestant woman in particular, the woman writer, the woman in the family, coping, hoarding, preserving, observing, keeping up appearances, seeing through the myths and hypocrisies, nursing the sick, conspiring with sister-women, possessed of a will to survive and to see others survive. (The southern black woman and the southern white woman share a history and a knowledge that we are barely on the edge of exploring.)

Welcome Eumenides reaches out from this scene yet has its roots there. The South is the only part of the United States to have lost a war and suffered the physical and psychic trauma of military defeat; this is another kind of knowledge that Eleanor Taylor, as a southern woman, possesses. The book ends with a long poem, "A Few Days in the South in February," which is the monologue or diary of a Yankee father going down to North Carolina at the end of the Civil War to find the grave of his son, exhume the body, coffin it, and bring it home for burial. The father's broodings are entirely personal yet they reveal the horror of war seen through the victor's eye devoid of machismo: The war is lost, for this father and for the others like him. In his forenote to the book, Richard Howard calls this "the best poem since Whitman about the War Between the States," and the fa-

ther Eleanor Taylor has recreated "from family papers" is Whit-
manesque in his compassion, determination and grief-stricken
dignity.

"After Twenty Years," another monologue on the aftermath
of another war, uses the voice of a woman in church: her son
was killed and buried in Normandy during World War II; her
husband has since committed suicide.

> My glove's rouge, with lipstick
> Or with teeth. . . . Curse *men*, curse *free* —
> God vault your freedom!
> Oh the acres of undistinguished
> Crosses make me sick.
> Mother could mark Papa's grave
> In the churchyard a mile from home,
> By its firs and shaft. . . .
> Your nothing grave . . .
> > Shame!
> . . . . .
> Give my son another life —
> A Norwood ugliness, a bourgeois rot,
> Dust and concrete, Falcons and Mustangs, not . . .

And there the poem ends. This mother does not pray, as the
Yankee father does, "I believe that the bounds of our lives/Are
fixed by our Creator . . ./Blessed be the name of the Lord." Her
grief is anger, a rebellious gnawing at gloved fingers; better her
son should *live* in the mean material postwar world than be dead
in one of those wars which men have rationalized to her, to
themselves.

But the truly remarkable poem in the book, one for which it
should be read even if it did not contain other strong poems, is
the title poem, "Welcome Eumenides." Out of the world and the
wars that men have made she conjures the voice of Florence
Nightingale, reliving her days and nights at Scutari, the death-
ward of the Crimean War, with glimpses back into the family-
centered, trivializing life of nineteenth-century English women
of the leisure class. (Many lines and phrases of the poem are di-
rectly quoted from actual notes Florence Nightingale left behind
her.) In this heroic, oral poem, densely woven and refrained, El-

eanor Taylor has brought together the waste of women in society
and the waste of men in wars and twisted them inseparably.

> Who calls?
> Not my child.
> (*O God no more love*
> *No more marriage*)
> Only my British Army.
> . . . . .
> (Where did I yawn
> In the face of the gilt clock
> Defying it to reach 10?)
> Stuff straw for deathbeds, for deathbeds,
> For deathbeds.
> Not one shall die alone.
> I die with each.
> Now hurry to the next lax hand, loose
> tongue,
> Quick messages for forever.
> Mr. Osborne knelt down for dictation.
> His pencil skirmished among lice.
> At last, the chance for a rich and true life.
> . . . . .
> I dreamed . . .
> Compulsive dreaming of the victim.
> The rich play in God's garden.
> Can they be forgiven?
> Their errors gambol scintillating
> Under the chandeliers like razors honed.
> I murder their heaven,
> I, *starving, desperate, diseased. . . .*
> ("You'll catch something and bring it home.")
> *Mother, you were willing enough*
> *To part with me to marriage.*
> No, I must take some things;
> They will not be given.

Florence Nightingale, well-born, beautiful, courted, living
out the rituals of society and the oppressions of the Victorian
family which held its daughters in a clutch of duty and hysteria;
becoming neurasthenic; battling her relations and her class to enter a profession considered demeaning and immoral; preparing
herself with heroic patience and in secret for the great occasion

which Victorian imperialism was eventually to provide her—
Eleanor Taylor has compressed what might be the materials for a
play or a film into eight intense pages of verse. The materials are
ideally suited to her style, a style born of tension, in which whispered undertones are in dialogue with the givens of social existence, with the sudden explosive burst of rebellion or recognition:

> A girl, desperately fortified in my castle,
> The starched pure linen,
> Scalded plates, the sanitary air,
> The facile word killed soul-ferment.
> Six courses starved the spirit.
> *And I said of laughter, mad,*
> *And of mirth, what is it doing?*
> I dreamed of all things at man's mercy.

Nightingale was, of course, no Victorian angel in the house but a
brilliant administrator and researcher, a fighter, with terrifying
endurance and a keen sense of politics. She was also a driven
woman; the split-second urgencies of her will come through in
the jagged lines and verse paragraphs of the poem.

What I find compelling in the poems of Eleanor Taylor, besides the authority and originality of her language, is the under-
lying sense of how the conflicts of imaginative and intelligent
women have driven them on, lashed them into genius or madness, how the home-nursing, the household administration, the
patience and skill in relationships acquired at such expense in a
family-centered life, became an essential part of the strength of a
woman like Nightingale, but at tremendous price. *Welcome
Eumenides* is a writing-large, in terms of a celebrated and powerful woman, of unanswered questions that hover throughout Eleanor Taylor's poems, and throughout the history and psychol-
ogy of women.

A Vase of Captured Light: The Poetry of Eleanor Ross Taylor

At the end of a recent poem, Eleanor Ross Taylor asks herself: "Shall I hum? Or sing/out clear?" Her hesitation articulates the dilemma at the heart of so many of this fine poet's poems. The struggle to sing out clear, to outwit the forces that encourage mere humming, emerges repeatedly in the poems as the tension between the domestic and visionary, between the local and the worldly, between convention ("concord with one's status quo") and the demands of the imagination. "Not yet, not yet," warns one of the poet's stern inner voices in "At the Altar." There is decided risk in opening the metaphoric bag in that poem—"that bag you packed me/when you sent me/to the universe"—at once a trousseau of manners and her own deferred poetic gifts. To unleash those gifts could be not only "hazardous to institutions"—it "could be fatal."

Risk erupts in the midst of the ordinary, as in the poem "Deer," when the poet, drinking with friends at twilight, observes two fawns—one male, one female. The male is skittish. "He paws and leaps and nears. She grazes on." In the fawns' split natures, in the liminal boundary between day and night, the poet senses "something targeting" her complacent evening. Within a matter of lines, the restless male deer is made to embody the poet's task:

> This something knows
> something it has to do—
> shatter a wall and jump through.

Like jumping through walls, to break the "boughs/of protocol," as she says elsewhere, to leave the reliable "highway" for the "jungle" of the imagination, is to risk getting injured or lost. She must remake her choice as often as doubt wells up; repeatedly, she forces herself to "proceed without a guide . . . though it's known madness."

She resists—has over and over again had to resist—the little deaths of etiquette, the hand-over-the-mouth of propriety. To be a poet is to be "unladylike" in the world Taylor paints, that "wilderness of ladies" for whom she titled her first book. Caught between social expectations and the lonely quest of poetry, she wonders if she "dare face my given garments." Fortunately, she has dared for decades.

The slow, jagged arc of Taylor's public career as poet suggests the patience of a long steeping, a rich absorption of language and experience. She has followed the advice she offers another in "To a Young Writer":

> Tuck your wits in,
> Say finally
> I did outdure them all

The shifting rhythm and bold declaration are vintage Taylor—reticence become toughness, hesitation become grace. She is like the namesake blackberry she finds in a gardening catalogue:

> Here's a
> variety called *Taylor*: "Season late,
> bush vigorous, hardy . . . free from rust."

Yet Taylor's determined re-awakening to poetry in old age still seems to put her life on the line: "I read somewhere/just waking up can kill you." The ever-looming mortality of the body spooks her: "I, past my expiration date," she notes drolly. Nevertheless she awakens herself early each morning and lets her durable imagination loose.

Here she is before dawn in "The Lighthouse Keeper," car lights rousing her—

> the long beams in the next drive
> cruising my hinterland,
> the safe slip of my single bed.

At once, the literal headlights enter the cauldron of half-dream and are imaginatively transformed into lighthouse lamps, the keeper "bringing the beams/home with her for the day" to illuminate the realm of kitchen and garage. For most poets that would be enough, the transformation of the ordinary into metaphor, the mundane eliding into the revelatory. But not content to leave those powerful beams at rest, Taylor further imagines that someday,

> snipping at the sink
> she'll hack them short
> and spike them in a vase
> for her window

—and now the visionary is domesticated into a bouquet of pure light, truncated, hacked to fit, but a beacon all the same. "Beware," she warns in conclusion. Poetry has occurred. The gap between the diurnal and the Orphic is momentarily bridged. Taylor's poems are like that vase of captured light—unexpected pairings, sudden pivots yielding illumination. The poems take form in what looks, at first, like inauspicious circumstances—"Sparrow Eats Fried Chicken Wing," "Cuts Buttons Off an Old Sweater"—and then they leap, like the fawn in "Deer," from ground level to the lofty in a few sculpted seconds.

The garden in which Taylor situates so many of her poems is no sanctuary from the world's ills (just as the domestic is no shelter or inhibition), but a diorama for the ceaseless struggle between eros and thanatos. Though it may easily slip into the mythic, it is very much an actual garden where she is bloodied by thorns, where she labors to prune, hoe, and transplant, to drive off insects and blight. The mortal art of gardening—where disease can "out-live host," where each summer's work withers away and is re-faced each spring—is an ideal tableau for the dramas Taylor is drawn to. There is always a trap door into life-and-death matters waiting to be happened upon, as in "The Accidental Prisoner," where, momentarily inattentive, she locks herself under her porch. Awaiting rescue—"Will anybody find me/under my own back porch?"—she journeys mentally from how "a Bastille/daylight lattices this cell" to the worry of a burner left on in the kitchen, from a pile of unused "stained, chipped flowerpots" at her feet to the captive's fear of hunger and thirst, until at last—

> I could have washed these pots
> and filled them with rosemary.
>
> Nota bene, my survivors: I'm to be buried
> in the old part of the cemetery.

The surprising slant rhyme and swiftness of the leap from anecdote to ultimate declaration is startling, but the canny movement and flinty gaze is something we can count on in Taylor's work. Mortality lurks at every turn. It is scried daily by her dogged, unsentimental eye. Laundry on the line turns into ghosts. Empty suitcases are "a fleet/of hearses headed for the attic." The bottom drops out of the normal with alarming rapidity and in rushes the existential.

As Jarrell wisely saw from the start, there is in Taylor's poems a "fault along which life divides, along which the earthquakes of existence occur." Hers is the poetry of "gaps, disparities, cleavages, discontinuities. . . ." Typical is the poem "Dust," where house dust is first literal dirt, an embarrassment, goblets "furred" with it, and a worrisome lapse ("How'd all those years/skip me?"). But within a couple of breaths, the poet recognizes the crater she's opened and arcs off in a knowing trajectory:

> dust kicked up from old rugs,
> dust of my daily tread
> sieved onto
> these-my-goblets,
> flatting their flash,
> ashing the Médoc's red,
> ashing my lips

Though taking on a musical life of its own that governs its downward spiral—an arpeggio of vowels and the syntactic refrain—the poem is characteristic of Taylor in its unflinching reach. Out of the seemingly trivial, she heads arrow-like for uncomfortable truths. "Who's this/I have invited?" she concludes the shrouded poem. Death is always on the tip of her tongue. It is not that she is habitually pessimistic. There is certainly a measure of joy in the poems: a treasured grandchild, the antics of a cat. In "Next Year," she embraces the future when "everything will be bigger," when there will be more time, more money, more knowledge—"I'll be a black forest of folk wisdom/floored with green cones." In "Love Knows," she swiftly sketches the "one story" of romantic love and concludes, "Luckily, it is my story." But she doesn't let down her guard against what can rupture health and happiness; she never hoods her eye.

Taylor's poems have grown sparer over the years but have suffered no loss in density. Her customary method is accretion: fragments of phrase, single words, deliberately accumulated, or a flurry of trochees and spondees, deftly orchestrated with line breaks and white space. Consider the opening of "Find Me,"

> by my trail of fragments,
>   stale crumbs,
>
>   green broken boughs
>   of protocol.
>   Footprints
>   all missteps.

Each line opens another possibility of meaning, line breaks and rhythm intensifying resonance. There is no room for slack in this poetics. Listen to the virtuoso opening of "Harvest, 1925":

> It took two nights to shuck the Hawfields' corn,
>   piled, foreskinned, altar high,
>   outside the crib.
> Lanternlight. Hard trolling motions.
> Dark pent-up communion,
>   with supper first, many
> women together, in church clothes
>   preparing food relentlessly
>   as if for some dread rite.

We are plunged into a world, lowered word by word, line by line, from the particular into the mythic dark. "Below the shuck

pile/was a paradise/lipped by wild plums/in troubled tangle."
The pace is pitiless, the looming erotic scandal inevitable as
Adam and Eve. We require only the quickest sketching in of
character and scene because of the evocative precision of each
chosen word: Big Helen Hawfields with her "long sultry
breasts" stalking the harvest table, filling the lanterns, "the long
wicks heavy/with combustible,/all the blurred brandy dreams/
in her outskirts/gathered in one drunk longing/for Tattoo's
broad body." It's as if the word "long" is to blame for it all! We
need no explanation, no narrative clutter. Within four lines, "his
Maggie found them there"—the moment explodes and passes,
leaves us breathless, unsettled.

Taylor can compress a whole life into a gesture or two.
There's tremendous presence in what's missing but vibrating
around the edges of the poems. She often forges a terse, poly-
phonic drama, sometimes layering in historical or familial
voices, or her own conflicting urges. In "Salting the Oatmeal,"
character is established with a single line: "She never used a
measuring spoon." Careless or instinctive, this she "poured salt
in her palm/and flung it in the oatmeal." Enough said; the poet's
gaze shifts: "Some days it rained all day./Some winters it never
snowed." If anything's amiss, it's merely the weather. But no, the
weather reveals the life: "Her second marriage might have
worked./What if she'd used a measuring spoon?" Yet, as
quickly as those lines call us to judgment, a larger context in-
trudes:

> The bombers flew over every night
> but she never had to be dug out.
> Sometimes she reached for the saltcellar.

Within nine lines—the saltcellar now suggestive of a bomb shelter—a complex biography emerges and claims our empathy. In a
mere nine lines more, Taylor lets the character speak for herself
and then swiftly closes down the poem:

> *When we were in Austria,*
> *Hans cadged petrol and passports*
> *from three countries. . . .*

> *We had to leave Herr Mohl behind.*
> *And my mauve accordion. . . .*

> When things were too salty
> she drank a glass of water
> or most anything.

From a seemingly random observation arises a life, the human response to extremity, a stark image of survival. Few poets can manage such a feat as succinctly. It takes not only craft, but decades of keen observation, thorough knowledge of one's terrain.

Eleanor Ross Taylor is *of* her terrain—the south, women's world within it—as few contemporary American poets are. She has a deep-sunk root in the several places she has lived, so there's an inherent *thereness* in the poems, the unmistakable imprint of her time and place and circumstance. She intimately knows and belongs to the world she was born into: "All, my mother said, in this backwoods/some kin to me." When a landscape is interwoven with relations, as hers is, when one lives within a genuine community, there is no abstracting of human foibles and woes, no stereotypes, but authenticities. Family is what hones her courage:

> for here warmth gathers in a fist,
> the fingers of one family, drawn up
> against destruction, knuckles knelt
> against indomitable season.

Taylor's language, too, is of its place, unhomogenized by the machine of pop culture. She is quirky in her syntax, bold with neologisms and compounds ("clock-stopped," "time-quaked," a "scissorly-wise drama," "kiss-me-quick-I'm-off-goodbye"). In this, she also represents a diminished quality in American poetry.

Yet she would not wish her place frozen in time, would not trade the unpredictabilities of life for stasis, as she affirms in "Va. Sun. A.M. Dec. '73," where abbreviations collude with the pace of time passing:

>things are disappearing forever
>   mtns. behind the mounting pines
>deer shot
>wedding rings flung in drawers
>Suns. no diff from rest of the wk.
>Va. no diff rest of the world
>
>In dead-land nothing changes.

She'll take her chances, suffer the losses, find consolations. She has, at age eighty, a steady hand at poetry's tiller, a gaze with no illusions, an unquenchable thirst. What a good guide she is.

Woman Singing: The Poems of Eleanor Ross Taylor

Wilderness of Ladies, Eleanor Ross Taylor's first collection, contains poems of unusually authoritative peculiarity and slightly more than moderate difficulty. The book appeared in 1960, when Modernism was still the most important force in the direction of Anglophone poetry, and when a woman could use the word "ladies" with perhaps a little less irony than it would usually carry now. Late Modernism in the American South, however, is laden with ironies, and with the evocation of voices, some ghostly. The twenty-eight poems here arise from a family history, and almost every one of them, as Geoffrey Hartman noted in an early review, "is a play of voices coming straight from the middle of the poet's world." The poet's world, as portrayed here, faintly suggests the gatherings of women that have become more frequent and celebratory in the last few decades, as women have done more about exercising the powers they share, and as men have gradually begun to let go of the notion that all women talk about in such gatherings is the pain of having men in their lives.

The women in these poems are those of a single community, a single extended family, but they are not gathered at some kind of regular empowerment session. They speak from several points in time, out of intense moments in their daily lives, including last moments on deathbeds. The effect of the collection, and of the intense lyricism of most of the poems, is to make all the voices just about equally present. Several generations are represented here, and occasionally a poem will contain a genea-
logical detail:

> My full name is Aminta Watkins Dunlap Ross.
> My mother was Merina Wilkerson.
> My father was Arnold Watkins—he carpentered—

These lines come at the end of the first section of "Family Bible," which concludes the book; the section characterizes "Uncle Mun,/A baroque buckle/Not to be undone." It is he who is responsible for this brief historical note, and yet the speaker's attitude toward that responsibility seems mixed:

> Was it not thoughtful of him
> On her busy death day
> As she counted quilt-blocks
> To elicit this data
> In Spencerian pencil
> Laid away in the clock
> For me,
> Posterity?

This is not a question that admits of a quick or easy answer. The information has its value, the piece of paper and the avuncular handwriting have theirs, yet there is the image of the hovering inquisitor, akin to the obtuse old gentleman in Wordsworth's poem who has trouble accepting the answer "We are seven."

Still, possession of such meager facts as these does not, in the end, always keep us informed of exactly where we are in the welter of voices arising from this gently clamorous book. Though these are poems, and extremely well-made ones, they maintain, for the most part, the narrative illusion that the speakers address informed listeners; so when one speaker addresses another and mentions "your Grandma," she probably means the Grandmother we encounter elsewhere. It is not immediately easy to be certain about this, but such uncertainty as there may be does not matter: the experience of the book is to be amidst the voices, lifted out of each of the specific times a voice comes from, into a present deeply enriched by the past.

Geoffrey Hartman's review singles out "Her Day" for special attention in this regard:

> The usual pattern is more erratic, words and
> quotes revealing a kind of geo-psychical faulting,
> as the person who is on the point of death (actu-
> ally or imaginatively) confuses cries of birth and
> of pain, salvation and doom, beauty and evil.

One of the finest minglings is in the poem "Her Day," where Grandmother's death is described as a passing over (the Styx), the waters being childhood memories sharp enough in the end to choke her.

Taylor reprinted this poem in *New and Selected Poems* (1983), but not in *Days Going / Days Coming Back* (1991), though it continues to reward patient attention. An unidentified speaker, perhaps a daughter or granddaughter, characterizes the day at the beginning of the poem:

> All day it had kept turning dark, like rain
> Coming, or like the day of the eclipse,
> When the cows had come up to the barn
> And bellowed to be milked.
> (If you could hear, for pain.)
> They hadn't known. Was it the Second Coming?
> *No, Granny, dear, it's not the end.*
> They looked in the almanac, later on.

The first sentence is in the pluperfect tense, and makes a cast even farther back, to "when the cows had come up." This temporal remoteness is countered by the immediacy of the images and the diction, with its two interruptions from different moments. The parenthetical aside appears to be in the speaker's present, but the italicized quotation takes us quickly back to the side of the deathbed, and the stanza ends with a statement about a later occurrence that is still in the past, from the speaker's point of view.

The second stanza is longer and portrays an increasingly blurred consciousness without losing clarity of impression. It begins with an idiomatic use of "now" with the imperfect tense that compresses time almost imperceptibly:

> Now the cows were surely at the bars.
> It was getting night, one might have known.
> Some of you get a bucket and go on!
> They prodded one another with their horns,
> (If you could see, for pain.)

> She sat up, fretted with a thread she'd torn.
> They low so pitiful! Go on!

As the stanza proceeds, the grandmother momentarily sees a small black child in the bedpost, and then she recalls, and imaginatively enters, her childhood:

> As children we played down at Cluster Rocks,
> On the river. Scary, it was—
> We played clubfist—
> Grab hold, Liza!

There follows a game-rhyme that ends with someone's being "O, U, T, out," and the grandmother comes to a new awareness:

> You play so mean, making grown women cry
> Old women. . . . No, death choked
> I'm there at last
> I'll cross the golden river
> The river that bright angel feet have trod. . . .

Both Geoffrey Hartman and Randall Jarrell, who provided a valuable introduction to *Wilderness of Ladies*, have noticed how many of these poems, like this one, move at their ends toward water, often in the form of the river—Styx, Jordan—one crosses to reach the afterlife. In this poem, the confluence of the river recalled from childhood and the river of death is managed with a graceful blend of pathos and humor. Immediately following the last quoted line above, there is an indented parenthetical passage of three lines that seems at first to refer back to "the golden river," but moves to an earthly consideration, made more so by the whiff of country speech:

> (Does the river look muddled to you?
> There's no fishing in March;
> Wait till the water's clare.)

In the last eight lines, the first of which uses "was here" as the first line of the second stanza uses "Now . . . were," it becomes difficult to separate all the strands woven into a vision—

the speaker's or Grandmother's—of uncles in a rowboat at Cluster Rocks, Charon crossing the Styx, a moment of tense earthly discomfort, a moment just at death, and a last look at this world or a first look at the next:

> Then Cluster Rocks, alight, was here:
> Behold! an old lady her uncles rowed across—
> The boat beneath her slipped the bank
> Just as she stepped ashore.
> "Stretched me arightsmart," she chirped.
> O to think of that dying!
> O unworthy "Stretchedmearightsmart"!
>
> She glared at hell through tears.

The constant yet shifting availability of the past as an important constituent of the present has rarely been portrayed with such concentrated skill. The book's title is a reminder that, though it might have been phrased "ladies in the wilderness," the accumulation of ghostly voices and the recurring moments of death make the present phrasing more accurate.

Indeed, there are a few poems here whose grim directness brings to mind the photographs in Michael Lesy's path-breaking *Wisconsin Death Trip*, which combines late nineteenth-century funeral portraits and contemporaneous newspaper accounts of madness, murder, and suicide. "In the Churchyard," for instance, takes a partial census of horror stories, in a voice almost comically glib:

> And there was Uncle Risdon.
> Married a Miss Catherine Tye. Aunt Catherine
> Somehow I can't now call her full name.
> She took a galloping consumption
> After she let the baby catch on fire.
> . . . . .
> And Cousin Mazeppa took laudanum.
> "Why did you do it, Zeppie, girl?
> Wa'n't Daddy good to you?"
> "Pray, let me sleep!"

In "Goodbye Family," the speaker enters the water of death of her own will, recalling how

> Every day I opened the drawer and
> Scanned the knives;
> Were there enough, sharp enough,
> For all lives?

"Song" opens with a variation on the collection's theme:

> Oh my dearie,
> Our childhoods are histories,
> Buckets at the bottom of the well,
> And hard to tell
> Whether they will hold water or no.

The speaker here is the grandfather, who recalls as one of the central events of his life his discovery of a corpse in the water near where he was plowing one day:

> It was in the paper with my name.
> I found him.
> I have the clipping tells all about it,
> If your Grandma aint thrown it out.
>
> Oh my dearie
> When our faces are swol up
> We will look strange to them.
> Nobody, looking out the door
> Will think to call us in.
> They'll snap their fingers trying
> To recollect our names.

Male speakers are scarce in this collection. The most prominent is "The Chain Gang Guard," whose situation parallels that of most of the women, in that he is somehow in charge, yet unable himself to escape. What holds him is a life he may have chosen, since his choice appears to him to have blocked others. That this situation is more typically that of women than of men is nowhere clearer than in "Woman as Artist" and "Sister," powerful evocations of female struggle for survival and identity. "Sis-

ter" recalls affections, games, and rivalries, the "wars of marriage and the family," but makes a dramatic declaration at the
end:

> And riding the trolley homeward this afternoon
> With the errands in my lap
> I would have disfestooned my world —
> A husband, more or less!
> A family, more or less! —
> To have alighted to a cup of kettle-tea
> And someone
> To whom I could lie merrily,
> Use malapropisms, be out-of-taste . . .
> . . . . .
> We'd play it solitary while the dusks rushed by,
> More than one flesh-and-blood,
> Almost one I.

"Woman as Artist" rattles the cage of motherhood:

> Kneel, fathers.
> If my babies are right,
> It is not because of you!
> Or me.

She poses a question as an answer:

> When I first gave the question life,
> The howling naked question life,
> Did I not have some inkling of the answer,
> And the answer answered,
> The door that closed across the room
> As my door opened?

Wilderness of Ladies ends with the sequence mentioned earlier, "Family Bible." The fifth section gives the granddaughter,
the poet, the last word. She recalls two encounters between herself and her grandmother; first, an indoor moment, in a dressing
room, when the granddaughter could have been more help than
she was; then, a recollection of Homecoming Day at Rehobath
Church, a few months before the grandmother's death, when the

grandmother approached in a majestic array of black dress and veils,

> And all my heart said,
> Run to her! Claim her!
> (Wild loneliness that
> Beats its wings on death)
> Then the spell broke.
> We who had waved across so many chasms
> No longer had to say we were not close.
> Was closeness more than painful separateness?
> We were a constellation of detached, like, ghosts.

One of the primary effects of *Wilderness of Ladies* is the merging of past and present by juxtaposing intense lyric moments from various points in time. In *Welcome Eumenides* (1972) this effect is not sought in nearly so unified a way, but the two most ambitious and interesting poems in the book make the past present by means of extending and sustaining lyric intensity over several pages of narrative.

The two poems are nearly equal in length—eight pages—and are based on historical material quite unequal in bulk. The first is the title poem, "Welcome Eumenides," which is a phrase Florence Nightingale entered in her diary. Taylor draws on Nightingale's diaries and on other biographical material from that long and distinguished life. The other poem is called "A Few Days in the South in February: A Hospitality for S. K. Wightman, 1865," and is "based," according to Taylor's note, "on Mr. Wightman's account of his pilgrimage to North Carolina reprinted from family papers in *American Heritage*, February 1963."

It is hard to know which of these projects presented the greater challenge. Stillman K. Wightman's narrative is extraordinary in itself, and recounts modestly and briskly a journey of heroic proportions. In about 15,000 words of artless but highly literate prose, Wightman reports on his round trip, between January 19 and February 8, 1865, between New York and Fort Fisher, North Carolina. His solemn purpose was to recover the body of his son, Edward, who had been killed January 15 in the Union attack on Fort Fisher, and bring it back home for proper burial. Despite many discouragements, that is what he did. The narrative is signed and dated March 4, 1865, so Wightman wasted no time in setting it down.

There is only one way to read this narrative without thinking of Priam's visit to the tent of Achilles, and that is not to have read *The Iliad*. Wightman makes no apparent move to remind us of this, though he quotes a letter from his son that makes parodic use of some images from the *Aeneid*. Taylor's opening lines do all that is necessary:

> One ship, one only
> One sentry
> One grave marked
>
> An old man seeking a battlefield,
> I march on the land of the enemy
> For my son.

This is not the place for a detailed examination of Wightman's very considerable achievement, but some indication of what he did might make it easier to see how Taylor has made use of his work in the process of making her own. Here are Taylor's lines based on Wightman's account of approaching the fort; they appear on the first and second pages of her poem, whereas Wightman has been telling his story for several pages at this point:

> The battlefield stretches south.
> Is it salt-marsh birds —
> Or dead soldiers whistling?
> Nightmare or real madness?
> I stumble over dead grass locked in ice.
>
> This alien wind blows sand
> Not southern; arctic sand peppers
> My flowing eyes and face.
> I hear my wild voice singing hymns;
> Feel tears like death-throes shake me,
> Then breath gives out and I sit down to rest.
> The salt wind roughs sand-wounds.
> The eye calls, *Edward*. . . .
> Answer, only those wind-borne birds.

Expanse of sea and marsh.
Expanse of dunes.

In 1865, Stillman Wightman was a successful attorney in New York, sixty-two years old. It emerges from his story that he was strong, decisive, devout, and resourceful. After almost ten days on trains and boats, he approached Fort Fisher on foot, from a landing near the mouth of the Cape Fear River some two miles away:

> The travelling was irksome, the wind was cold and cutting, and came sweeping from the north-west over Cape Fear River, and the salt marsh and sand beach with irresistible rush; and by the time I had walked one half the distance, my frame began to quiver, and I felt that the days of my youth were gone. . . .

He spends a paragraph on the difficulty, still to be solved, of locating the body and identifying it, and thinks despairingly of the custom of mass graves.

> These doubts and difficulties, and my well nigh exhausted condition, all had a strong tendency to almost dishearten me, until the pressure of my feelings began to find vent in tears. At first I thought I would sit down and rest, but I was in the midst of a salt marsh, and that was impracticable. Next, I sought for some spot where I might be partially shielded from the cold, cutting wind; but there was not any place any where near me to afford the least relief. It was at this time that my heart broke forth in prayer to God, to strengthen and nerve my mind and body, and enable me to perform what I had undertaken, if it could be consistent with His holy will. Almost at the same instant, the promises of God came into my thoughts with great force and energy. "As thy days, so shall thy strength be." "Fear not, for I am with thee." "I will never leave thee nor forsake thee."
> Other passages of similar import came into my mind, until I was comforted, and became joyful,

and exclaimed aloud in the language of the
Psalmist, "The Lord is my shepherd, I shall not
want;" and then I commenced and sang the
hymn—

> *The Lord my shepherd is*
> *I shall be well supplied,*
> *Since he is mine and I am His,*
> *What can I want beside.*

I would walk and sing till my breath began to
fail, and then stop and rest, and then again, walk
and sing.

Aside from the obvious difference in bulk—Wightman does
in three hundred words what Taylor does in eighty-eight—there
are the details Taylor has omitted, and those she has added,
from her own knowledge of coastal North Carolina, and her de-
cision to have Wightman sit down to rest. He uses the perfect
tense, she the present. The chief difference, though, is that Taylor
has made a poem, and Wightman a prose narrative. The significance of this simple distinction is well expressed in Richard
Howard's introductory note to *Welcome Eumenides*, when in connection with this poem he mentions Taylor's being the wife of
Peter Taylor, whose achievement in prose can help to show her
what hers must be in verse: "Whereas the prose voice rubs itself
out as it goes along, her voice must be somehow suspended,
held up on its rhythms, its intervals, its silences, until no message is left but a resonance, no communication but an echo: persistent, yielding, heard."

Taylor's speaker is, in short, not the same speaker as Wightman's. He partakes of a voice and manner that she gives him,
though she draws heavily on his narrative and quotes him
briefly a few times. This is a technique that, in the Western tradition as we have so far recovered it, makes its first great appearance in the Greek tragedians' derivations from Homer. One may
read each of the works several times, taking each on its own
terms (the poem's terms including, to be sure, its acknowledgment of indebtedness), finding more and more of their disparate
excellences.

This poem, too, displays a strong sensitivity to temporality. Wightman's prose is relatively careful with the details of the clock and the calendar, and Taylor picks up a few of his references to time in the early parts of the poem. She quotes from Edward's response to the family's Christmas letter, and she has Wightman ask where to find "Graves from the battle of January 15." Subsequent references to time become much more subjective. At Edward's grave, Wightman stands transfixed. "It seems I may spend out my years/Beside the spot." He walks away toward the fort three times, and returns to mourn. When he approaches the commanding officer about exhumation, he is at first put off:

> Take up the body now?
> Only a pine coffin? Ah.
> At some future time. . . .
> With one of lead. . . .

Days pass into night without being counted carefully. The materials required are gathered, the body is exhumed, identified, wrapped and coffined, brought home

> To services appropriately grave.
> There lie in peace till Morning.
> The sent-out child lies harvested.
> The stone doves peck.

> My watch ticks in my waistcoat.
> My *News* waits by the window.
> Snow falls
> *I believe that the bounds of our lives*
> *Are fixed by our Creator*
> *And we cannot pass them.*

The poem ends with a tableau composed of images of stasis, eternity, and the mundane daily measurement of time: from Judgement Day to the daily *News*. The unpunctuated transition from the imagined voice to the final quotation is like a freeze-frame shot as the voice-over continues, keeping us in the extended present of this splendid poem.

Florence Nightingale's life, too, was long, and richly adorned with great achievements. Taylor's poem, "Welcome Eumenides," can neither compress the whole of the life within its compass, nor restrict itself, as the Wightman poem does, to a single episode. Instead it recreates a wandering consciousness whose fragmentary and often transitionless shifts of mood and scene are made more plausible and compelling in the light of the recollection that Nightingale's own apparent grasp of the world around her deteriorated in her last few years.

The poem is anything but incoherent, however, and is set at a time in Nightingale's life when she was still the alert and incredibly well-organized administrator who is sometimes hidden by the legendary glow of "The Lady With the Lamp." Nightingale was a tireless record-keeper, maker of stern rules, reporter of hard facts: the only page of this poem that does not contain at least one numerical quantity does use the word "statistics." Early in the poem, however, Taylor quotes for the first of three times a diary entry: "*O God no more love/No more marriage.*" By using this as a kind of refrain, Taylor suggests sublimation as a source of some of Nightingale's vast energy, but the overall effect of the poem is to expose, in order to deepen, the mystery of Nightingale's devotion, and that of war's incomprehensible waste.

Though both Wightman and Nightingale make numerous expressions of faith in God, and though both are tragically involved with the wastes of war, it is significant that Wightman is chiefly concerned with one casualty, and Nightingale with thousands. That men and women relate differently to war is an oversimplification and a cliché; like both of those modes, it has its kernel of truth. In this poem, Nightingale has little to say about battle itself, and nothing about victory. By way of reminding us of General Sherman's brief unforgettable characterization of war, Taylor has Nightingale say, "And then, all Balaclava broke loose."

A far more direct feminine excoriation of war occurs in "After Twenty Years," the second poem in the book. It is the monologue of a woman whose son died in the Normandy invasion, and whose husband has since taken his own life. "Curse *men,*

curse *free*," she says, and bewails "the acres of undistinguished/
Crosses." At the end of the poem, she calls up a life of almost
aggressive ordinariness as infinitely preferable to such death:

> Give my son another life —
> A Norwood ugliness, a bourgeois rot,
> Dust and concrete, Falcons and Mustangs, not . . .

Norwood could be — not just anywhere, but maybe one of the
corroded studs on the Rust Belt, or a backwater southern town,
where these Falcons and Mustangs fall far short of wild majesty.

The paring-down of *Welcome Eumenides* — fourteen poems
omitted from it in *New and Selected Poems*, four more in *Days Going / Days Coming Back* — serves to throw into sharper relief another recurrent concern of these poems, which is the speaker's
connection with nature, especially trees. Most of the dropped
poems are brief and notational, recording encounters with day-
to-day life, always expertly, sometimes satirically, but not always memorably. Among the remaining poems is "Courtesy
Call, 1967" (the comma has been added to the title since *Welcome
Eumenides*), which sidles right up next to disastrous sentimental-
ity and stays there for a page without falling over the edge. It is a
direct address to a tree, a landmark along a stream where the
speaker spent long hours in childhood. Now the landscape is
overgrown, the stream sluggish, the swimming hole silted in.
The poem saves itself by means of precise description and an
ending that contains a small but effective surprise:

> Except that you've grown truly ancient . . .
> I? The same.
> The same, and elderly.
> Like you trapped in some far neglect;
> Reflections deepened, dulled,
> Our voices out.

Forms of the word "trap" become more noticeable in Taylor's more recent work than they are in her first two books,
though constraint is a major theme from the beginning. In the
group of new poems first gathered in *New and Selected Poems*,
there is another longer poem inspired by a historical document.

"Rachel Plummer's Dream" is based on the narrative of Rachel Plummer herself, whose life was short, but eventful and difficult. Born in Illinois in 1819, she married at 14, moved to Texas and bore a son. In 1836, when she was seventeen and pregnant with her second child, she was captured by Comanches and held as their slave for thirteen months. Her second child, born in captivity, was brutally killed when he was about six weeks old. In June of 1837, she was ransomed by a group of Mexicans and reunited with her husband early in 1838. Though she was "emaciated, covered with scars, and in very poor health," she very soon became pregnant again, giving birth to her third child on January 4, 1839. On March 19 of that year she died, and the child died two days later. Despite her trials, she was able to write an account of them, which was published in Houston in 1838.

The title of that text is *Rachael Plummer's Narrative of Twenty One Months Servitude as a Prisoner Among the Comanchee Indians*. Taylor looks briefly but clearly at the horrifying facts of Plummer's suffering, but saves for special consideration an odd episode partly factual, partly dreamed, in which Plummer enters a cavern and has visions. The poem, unlike the two longer ones in *Welcome Eumenides*, is in the second person, the better to address Plummer's own indomitable interest in her plight and her surroundings. Taylor portrays her as a woman who was bound to see what there was to see, numbed though she was with fatigue and pain, driven at last toward a vision of the sort that saints have had, including a sense of her child's voice and a Being who salves her wounds:

> How analyze
>   this parapsychologic episode
>   this spiritual hiatus where
> you closed your eyes a whole day and a night,
> on through a second day?—
>   I discount sex.
> So worn, half-starved, and suicidal—
>   they say, consumptive, too.
> The realist, you painted not at all.
>
> I see him, see his gifts. He chose: to bathe
> your wounds that never pained again,

> that Resurrection flaring in the cave,
> those stars in earth, time stopped
> and you with eyes to see.

This poem is followed by the last poem reprinted in *Days Going*, "In the Bitter Roots." In it, a roving consciousness focuses briefly on a rapid sequence of scenes, like a bird in a room, flying from one window to another. The mountain range in Idaho and Montana indicated by the title is usually spelled as a single word; separating "bitter" and "roots" suggests contemplation of difficult origins. "They think me dead," the speaker says; yet it is hard to be sure whether the speaker is a possibly identifiable historical personage, or a representative of the poet's consciousness. There is regret in the realization that one will not now ever cross the Mississippi, or stand with Lewis and Clark, or participate in the trials of Rachel Plummer, but is

> Only to stand watching
> the chimneys take the sun . . .
> . . . . .
> trapped in these mountains
> trapped in this face. . . .

The poem ends with reference to the poems about Nightingale and Plummer as risky but possibly rewarding ways of getting somewhere:

> Can I think to find
> a past, a past self, in these passes,
> in hospital at Sevastopol,
> following among Comanche squaws?
> Yes, and more,
> I proceed without a guide
> at this stage of the expedition
> though it's known madness.

Days Going / Days Coming Back opens with a section of fifty-four poems under the title "Next Year." In these, and in the fifty-five poems in her most recent book, *Late Leisure* (1999), Taylor bears down more often on the immediacy of her own life as it draws toward — and then, according to "Late Leisure," beyond —

its "expiration date." The tone is sometimes elegiac, as the deaths of friends and loved ones come more often, children become aging adults, ordinary tasks become more challenging. References to confinement and constraint continue to be plentiful. As she says near the end of the multivoiced "War Paint and Camouflage,"

> Life's no longer simple.
> The hunger of the first part
> sues the hunger of the second part.

But there is also in many of these poems a humorous wisdom, a keen-edged wit that usually stays this side of satire through the power of abiding love.

"Short Foray" begins with a yellow jacket in a taxi, disturbing the speaker with visions of anaphylactic shock and death, disturbing the driver not at all: "he idled lassitudinously,/one with the motor." The second half of the poem muses on the coffee-stain on the speaker's blouse, the store-wrapped gift for an infant grandchild, the mysterious preferences of the daughter, who "likes new knaveries:/lentil pilaf, home videos." It ends with a meditation on the yellow jacket's purpose:

> Did he know it was October, bees-up time,
>   and take this warm day for a last rich look
>   at the boundaries of things, a day of
>   stinging a boundary or two if he felt like it,
>   playing time bomb?

In "One Sort of Heaven," Taylor considers the old consolation that after one's own death, one lives on in people's recollections, for a while. This seems reassuring, maybe, until Taylor reminds herself and us that some of these people will not enjoy the recollection any more than she enjoys remembering her old college advisor, Miss Magnhilde Anders, "rubbing her red wig/over her clammy forehead,/her glasses crustacean sockets."

Days Going ends with a seven-page poem called "Casting About," a rambling meditation on fishing. It takes its epigraph from a notice posted at Cross Creek Fish Camp: "At Cross Creek

Bill Long limited on bass Wed. A.M. using a purple floating worm." The poem begins, "To limit on something!" and plays with the ideas there—achieving limits, verbing nouns—and gradually moves toward irresoluble dualities, such as the enjoyment of cooked fish and horror at the caught fish's suffering. All the while, there is just below the surface of the poem the realization that this is traditionally male territory. Cautious of polemic but aware of where she is, Taylor makes no more of this than the poem itself, but that is a powerful sufficiency.

Just glancing at the table of contents in *Late Leisure* reminds us how things close in on the desire to break free: "Retired Pilot Watches Plane," "Completing the Pilgrimage," "A Change of State," "The Accidental Prisoner," "Always Reclusive," "One Last Warm Day," "The Hostage." "A Change of State" makes rueful fun of waking as a kind of transformation. The speaker comes to consciousness, because of a sound, a felt presence, or merely enough sleep:

> How do I? Not on purpose.
> Calm surprise, a flower unclosed.
>
> A fine flower,
> one foot in the grave,
> stiff ankle, unsteady leg . . .
> . . . . .
> I read somewhere
> just waking up can kill you.

Among the most adventurous of these new poems is "Contemplating Jailbreak," which is so fragmentary and private in its imagery that it makes its powerful statement as if by magic. It begins thus:

> Through the bars?
> surrender
> saw my music?
> scissors my embroidery?
> I was making masks for a rabbit
> using the bag the river came in
> a few holes
>
> marriage was an economy all round

I do not recognize immediate domestic origins of "masks for a rabbit" or "the bag the river came in," but they seem to have come into a dream by way of some ordinary activities. It is not quite the same kind of inadvertent surrealism that arises from such language as "Initialize the mouse on your Powerbook," but it is close. The dream of flight, the magic carpet beside the bed, has its childhood source:

> my testimony is
>   in the beginning
> my bed had
> little round china rolling feet
> that's why

Though this poem is in very sparsely punctuated free verse, the convergence of the child's voice and the adult's sympathy is like that in the best of *A Child's Garden of Verses*. I will remember those china rolling feet as long as I remember yellow candlelight.

Many years ago, reviewing *Wilderness of Ladies* for *Poetry*, X.J. Kennedy found himself mildly annoyed by Taylor's calm and easy willingness to alternate between metrical and unmetrical verse. (Would he have used the word "verse" there? I do, anyway.) Later, in a jacket comment for *Welcome Eumenides*, Allen Tate said, ". . . she is a formalist in a mode that must be described as epigrammatic lyricism." Formalism, indeed, does not require meter, but only some principle, preferably discoverable some of the time, according to which lines are arrived at. There are countless examples in which there is nothing more to point to than the rightness of the lines, the futility of rearranging them. That Taylor can write this way most of the time, and write metrically some of the time without inviting invidious comparisons, is a testimony to the depth of an artist's resources and to her devotion to the craft. She has made a remarkable number of strong and durable poems, and she is still at it. The Summer 1999 *Southern Review* contains two of her recent poems, one of which especially is both harrowing and consoling. "How to Live in a Trap" is cast as advice to the wild animal with a steel trap on its leg, and manages the extremely risky device of giving itself away in the last line:

You'll hear the wren sing
 procedure, procedure, proceed.
  If you pass out, dream a few days.

Lick wounds regularly.
 Practice deep breathing at scheduled
  intervals.

Tell yourself there's a painting
 in this somewhere:
  Interior, Woman Singing.

from "Structural Subversion"

There must be books available which explain in convincing detail why the South is, as Flannery O'Connor says, "a storytelling section." Sometimes what the observer means is a society's civil comportment: grocery traffic halts at the check-out counter while the employee at the register pauses to *tell the story* of her aunt's surgery to the customer next in line. Sometimes what is meant is fiction's dominance over poetry in the Southern canon, not only in the early and Confederate South but following the "Modern Renaissance." The Scott, Foresman anthology—the text for my college class in Southern Literature in 1963, as it probably was for my professor, at Vanderbilt a decade earlier—selects from four "Poets and Critics" since 1918: John Crowe Ransom, Donald Davidson, Allen Tate and Randall Jarrell. For "Prose Fiction" of the same period: Ellen Glasgow, Stark Young, Elizabeth Madox Roberts, Katherine Anne Porter, Caroline Gordon, Andrew Lytle, Jesse Stuart, Eudora Welty, Carson McCullers, Peter Taylor, Truman Capote, Flannery O'Connor and Shirley Ann Grau. Richard Wright shows up in a cultural commentary section, and the "Three Representative Authors" which end the volume are Thomas Wolfe, William Faulkner, and Robert Penn Warren, the last represented by two stories and four poems (including the thoroughly narrative "Ballad of Billie Potts").

If there is in the region a cultural compatibility with narrative, the imbalance in its literature seems natural enough. Narrative since Homer, lacking epic subject, has increasingly found a better location in fiction, where there is room to develop and reveal character over time, acting and acted upon. Making character known also needs idiom, and prose more easily sustains the idiomatic; all those unstressed syllables in speech rhythms—by the pond, under the tree, picking up the knife—and in poetry, whose first allegiance must be to music, nothing wears so quickly as the flat line. But Southern writers have also been instrumental in the wholesale reemergence of narrative in contemporary American poetry, restoring an audience for it by the by, and any recent anthology of Southern Literature contains their work: James Dickey, Fred Chappell, Dave Smith, James Applewhite, David Bottoms, Henry Taylor, David Huddle, Rodney Jones, Leon Stokesbury, T.R. Hummer, Andrew Hudgins, Brooks Haxton, and others. Definition follows practice; additional application follows definition. Even this sketchy account is, of course, itself a kind of story—How Southern Poetry Got To Be So Narrative.

So what does that make Charles Wright, Donald Justice, A.R. Ammons and Eleanor Ross Taylor, besides the exceptions to prove the rule? Out on a far branch of the family tree, wasn't there some subversive progenitor?

> Once upon a midnight dreary, while I pondered,
>   weak and weary,
> Over many a quaint and curious volume of for-
>   gotten lore,
> While I nodded, nearly napping, suddenly there
>   came a tapping
> As of some one gently rapping, rapping at my
>   chamber door.
> "'Tis some visitor," I muttered, "tapping at my
>   chamber door—
> Only this and nothing more."

It's a ghost story, of course, and also a prototype for current "personal narrative" in American poetry. Poet-speaker is up late reading, or trying to read, grieving actually for "the lost Lenore," rare and radiant—and dead—maiden. Bird knocks at the window, speaker lets him in, and conversation ensues (more or less—the bird really doesn't hold up his end, although the progressive hysteria of the speaker compensates). The structure here is didactic: from the fairy-tale opening to the last "Nevermore," almost every stanza carries at least one direct time reference ("midnight," "bleak December," "now," "presently," "Soon again," "Then," "Then," "Then," "Then") and one action ("I wished," "I stood repeating," "I opened wide the door," "I whispered," "I heard," "I flung the shutter," "Raven . . . perched" and "sat").

But Poe has built a fort to house a butterfly: there is no "story": nothing happens. Look at the predicates, once the bird enters: "quoth," "marveled," "spoke," "muttered," "said," "cried," "quoth," "said," "implore," "quoth," "said," "quoth," "shrieked," "quoth": once the bird enters, what follows is the rising line of despair and its corollary, the increasingly maddening vacuity of the bird's non-response. That the Raven doesn't peck him, or say anything else, or fly away, is what keeps it an emblem of both the speaker's distress and the failure of the world, civilized and natural, to alleviate that distress. Meanwhile, Poe's obsessive, sound-drunk ear provides the claustrophobic emotional field, having doubled the ballad conventions: the characteristic four-beat metric and its trimeter variation are recalled by interior rhymes ("dreary"/"weary," "napping"/"tapping"), the end rhymes are kept in the traditional alternating pattern ("weary"/"lore"/"tapping"/"door"), and the refrain hammers its one note—Nevermore—like a Chinese water torture. Despite its rigid narrative gestures, "The Raven" is lyric in its deepest purposes, and "our cousin, Mr. Poe," as Tate called him, the wellhead I was looking for in what I've come to think of as structural subversion.

Sequence, subsequent, consequence—the root is "to follow." Narrative can depart from or rearrange chronology but always plays against the presumption of its stability. If lyric structure fixes points on a graph, narrative fills in the line between them, on which to hang discursive information. Flannery O'Connor said, "[I]n a story something has to happen. A perception is not a story. . . . " But perception is precisely the lyric poet's gift, and the lyric poem may be said to be, in fact, "one perception immediately followed by another." To grasp this difference clearly, look closely at structure in microcosm, which is to say syntax:

> You were younger than last year,
> Younger than the day we were married,
> Younger than the day we met.

That's narration—expository information about character that also informs event and, indirectly, the narrator.

What are you doing?
To whom are you smiling?
Where are you going?
Will you not answer me?
Answer! Answer!

That's lyric, non-discursive and music-derived. Nothing is re-
vealed about the "you" except its silence, but the passage in-
structs us in what to feel—uncomprehending abandonment. Do
you hear how regular rhythm functions there, with the persistent end-stopped dimeter, the syntactical repetition, the small
variation ("What," "to whom," "where," "will you not"), the
echoed word? It's the same triad played in all its inversions.
Here's the full text of Eleanor Ross Taylor's ghost story, "Night":

I spent the night in Chastelton.
The splitting damasks hung in belts;
Those faded colors we admired
Forgot themselves in gray.
Light spider-bagged the baseboards, tired.
I climbed up to the children's room.
I knew the way.
Up steps and past a blistered stile
Along that thick oak balustrade
(You like old things? Behold!)

The carved door hung ajar.
I pushed it wide.
The birds flew from their roosts
And disappeared like mice into the sky.
Below, the garden that one time
Held itself clipped urns, hens, cones,
Of evergreen, had turned
A calendar of wastes,
A zodiac of despairs.
There was somebody there.

It was you.
You were a mortal sheen
Flickering from the negative.
You were younger than last year,
Younger than the day we were married,
Younger than the day we met.
What are you doing?

To whom are you smiling?
Where are you going?
Will you not answer me?
Answer! Answer!

Grief has one great wish and an eager imagination. The speaker has a vision, tries to get some answers, grows increasingly agitated—no raven here but a fair substitute in that "mortal sheen/Flickering from the negative," and an overt narrative structure, space measuring time:

I climbed up to the children's room.
Up steps and past a stile
Along the balustrade.
I pushed the door open,
The birds flew from their roosts.

Straightforward actions rendered in straightforward declarative (what I think of as narrative, because driven by subject and action verb) syntax. But Taylor is almost always sly. The storyline as I compressed it is boring; her poem is not. From the beginning, the linguistic energy resides not in the predicates that carry narrative but the descriptive asides:

The splitting damasks hung in belts.
Light spider-bagged the baseboards, tired.
The birds . . . disappeared like mice into the sky.
A calendar of wastes,
A zodiac of despairs.

These renderings form the true plot line—or at least a parallel line not chronological but musical, which is to say, plotted along degrees of intensity: crescendo, thickening chords. And how does she render the central narrative action? Without action: "There was somebody there./It was you." Then nothing but copulative verbs, shifting into present tense, then future tense as she refuses to report but enacts:

You were . . .
You were . . .

What are you doing?
To whom are you smiling?
Where are you going?
Will you not . . . ?

and the final imperative echoing into the white space: "Answer!
Answer!"

But Taylor has more complicated and subtle uses for structural subversion, particularly in her more recent poems, such as "Where Somebody Died":

The self refuses to appear
    in this bare place.
It fears that mute chair
    and the still window.
The sunlight scares it.
There might rise up a sound.
The door doesn't like to move,
    and the crow out there
    hesitates; he knows
    a hole flown into by mistake
    would make a bite of him.
What was sits standstill in the chair,
    hangs, stunned, against the dry-eyed light.
Nobody in sight.
Inanimate things, still lifeless.
This room's so empty
    I doubt I'm standing here;
    there can't be room for me
    and total emptiness.
Only some far-off sounds persist.
The brute truck
    over on the interstate.
The flames in the incinerator
    chewing his old vests.

This poem is the very inverse of "Night." Narrative information is limited to the title and the title's shading of the poem's first three adjectives ("bare," "mute," "still") and last four lines. Unlike the broad camera angle that opens "Night," we begin here in closeup, with unadorned, undifferentiated "self," "chair," "window," "door." Instead of a cast of characters or even a companion "I" — the neutrality of objects as protagonists;

instead of narrative distance afforded by past tense—present tense verbs. "Night" opened with description and moved, by way of simple action, to confrontation. The predicates here are internal, conditional, intransitive or simply omitted—look at the pivot, where the poem's only two concrete action verbs ("sits," "hangs") are smothered, stunned, and followed by sentence fragments:

> What was sits standstill in the chair,
>   hangs, stunned, against the dry-eyed light.
> Nobody in sight.
> Inanimate things, still lifeless.

Where ARE we? Who is telling this? The answer comes almost as an aside, again abstracted, and without any new narrative information:

> This room's so empty
>   I doubt I'm standing here;
>   there can't be room for me
>   and total emptiness.

The function of the lines, I think, is merely to insert the idiomatic "I," a fast glimpse of the recording sensibility. Merely? What an enormous shift in the tonal ground the lines create. Then back to the generalized, "objective" and intransitive—"Only some far-off sounds persist" —and more fragments:

> The brute truck
>   over on the interstate.
> The flames in the incinerator
>   chewing his old vests.

Because these last five nouns are so particular, and because the context has been so generalized ("place," "chair," "window," "door," "What was," "emptiness," "sounds," "room" used in both its meanings), the truck, interstate, and incinerator intrude with tremendous violence (enough to suggest this "somebody" might even have been killed on the highway, if our appetite for story is high).

If ever a poem proved the elusive point, this is it: music and feeling amplified within a suggested narrative frame. Think of its cousin, that pure lyric, "After great pain a formal feeling comes" — "pure" because the reader is divorced from narrative context, and even narrative speculation, in the very first line, one article or pronoun suppressed, the other indefinite. But what interests Taylor is how the chill, the stupor, coexist with the quotidian (sunlight, noisy traffic), as what interests her is almost always not the fixed moment of before/after that is the lyric's province, but how before/after, past/present, then/now continually bleed into one another. In "Where Somebody Died" the narrative suggestions of the title create an expectation for narrative which the predicates and impersonal pronouns deflect, even as they signal duplicity: this speaker only pretends to be omniscient, impersonal; we discover as the poem unfolds, from the personified door and crow, from the blurted first-person pronoun, from the penultimate adjective ("brute truck") and the final possessive ("his old vests"), a speaker clearly connected emotionally to the "Somebody" of the title. The poem is made of the tension between the suppressed particular story—who died, how he died, his significance to the speaker—and the common reactive grief/terror/guilt which usually seeks resolution in elegy. Narrative serves action, event, passage of time, revelation of character, but nothing happens here, and the poem is in part about that lack, a ghost story in which there is no ghost, in which time doesn't pass (or heal any wounds either). Try rearranging the order of the sentences: no external logic or sequence is violated, but doing so ruins the poem's shape, and its shapeliness, and our participation in its emotional field; and ruins the way establishing self, door and crow as dramatic personae allows absence to become one too; and ruins the text's unity and sonority, in which loss registers on sensibility. The poem's indelible impact is in its song, the flames "chewing his old vests" as long as the ink stays on the page.

A plot line, then, of sounds, of feeling. In music, one speaks easily of "line"; each note, even repetitions of the same note, must contribute to the phrase, which builds and subsides in volume or pitch or intensity, and each phrase must relate likewise to the others in the overall structure of the piece. "Where Somebody Died" is far from static: there is movement and energy in the phrasing, from the neutral, objectified *self* to the cautious crow; from the passive "There might rise up a sound" through "inanimate things, still lifeless"; from "The door . . ." through the "total emptiness"; from the first set of sentence fragments through the last; and all contribute to the arc stretching from the title through the burning vests.

What carries these progressions, or phrases, into the reader's right brain, bypassing the discursive habit of language, is the texture of repeated sounds, as tightly woven, albeit less regular, less predictable, as Poe's. To analyze Taylor's, we might first locate all the direct repetitions, as graph points: "still," "sound[s]," "chair," "there," "room," "stand," "empty." Then find other repetitions—full rhyme ("bare/chair/scares/there," "window/crow/knows/hole/flown"), half rhyme ("sunlight/might rise/like/bite," "refuses/mute/move/room," "place/hesitates/mistake/flames"), and all the drone notes—all the *s* sounds, the initial *st*s, the *l*s, *m*s, the short *i*. What's left? "Truck."

Of course, a texture this thickly chorded can't carry a great deal of narrative information with any clarity. And some readers may miss the inexorable momentum of narrative: this happened, and then this happened, and running parallel what might have happened—had not the crop been ruined, if the train had come on time. Narrative literature amplifies this aspect of "life story," each fork in the road foreclosing options, opening new ones, making our story ours. In Warren's "The Ballad of Billy Potts," we know the stranger is the murderers' son long before they do: if only they had lifted the victim's shirt and seen the birthmark . . . That tension between potential and actual makes a story compelling.

However, as storytellers know, this linearity is only physiologically and retrospectively true: it isn't really "like life" since it isn't how we experience life. Only after crisis do we see, or think we see, how one thing led to another, how circumstance developed out of prior circumstance and choice and event (which is why past tense is so compatible to narrative). And not even physiologically true. We have the bodies of children, then adults.

We have parents, then we don't. We live however long, then we're gone.

The relation of the writer to narrative material is always looking back down a one-way street—even if she has to imagine the future to look back from—and the idea of continuity, of chronology as an allegedly stable external referent, is a matter of temperament, faith and imagination: *there must be some good reason why this happened.* Which makes narrative, with its allegiance to sequence and continuity, with its illusion of significance and order, as much a manipulation of experience as the lyric's isolation and examination of moments of extreme emotional dilemma.

Presume the classifiers have it right: that the dominant gene in Southern poetry is narrative, that we are born to its structure as Chomsky says we are born to syntactical patterns, or that we inherit a taste for it with our corn bread and collard greens, or develop one from long hours with the *Old Testament*, rocking on the porch with relatives, or walking the stubblefield with a gun on the shoulder, looking for doves. Presume even that the "Southern materials"—family, land, the past—require a linear, discursive structure. The danger is that the opposite becomes equally operative: seeing no other structure, we may limit our subjects to those it most naturally serves, or assume significance where there is none, or write the poems already better written, or overprivilege regional idiosyncrasies. A good poem eludes formulae, and the danger in assumptions—for the writers of a region, or an ethnic group, or a gender, or even a period—is their risk of prescription. Corrupted structure can serve as a useful impediment, a "resisted motion," to borrow Warren's term, the grit provoking the pearl. Taylor's extraordinary formal inventiveness, her angle of vision, her acute eye, are not of course to be duplicated. But she imparts a great permission to other narrative-fostered, narrative-fated Southerners.

Rosanna Warren

"Don't Shiver": Poems of Eleanor Ross Taylor

Eleanor Ross Taylor's poems create their own electromagnetic field. They hum, sizzle, jolt, slide: the energy they produce almost dislocates syntax, setting nouns and adjectives throbbing with the force of verbs. Yet her poems charge up syntax only because of, and through, their intense syntactic knowingness. In the same spirit, they send high voltage Modernist verse freedoms buzzing along the wires of traditional cadences. These are poems, I am trying to say, completely alive and completely disciplined.

They have always been so. Her first book, *Wilderness of Ladies* (1960), already turned New Critical compactness and wit into highly individuated, off-kilter, risky feats (and fits) of engineering. Unlike other rebellious poems of the 60s, Taylor's poems accomplished themselves not through abandoning compactness and wit, but by commandeering them for private purposes. "Bemiracled rose, I see my cutting took," starts "The Bine Yadkin Rose" with characteristic Taylor zing and archness. These early poems do seem, in their fashion, cuttings from the great traditional stems of Donne and Marvell ("Till the round earth's ringed with Babel trumpets,/Some dark, some light./Some streakèdy," slyly predicts "Woman as Artist" of her plant "babies"). "Cutting," for Taylor, implies a sharp wounding that will give birth to new and related life: it perfectly describes her own relation to poetic tradition.

Irreverent rhyme ("Mamma"/"drama" from "The Bine Yadkin Rose"), concentrated diction and images, a streakedy prosody, give these early poems their substantial life. It is a life at once aware of limitation in human hopes and verse architecture ("They set a fiery candle in a teacup") and of mortal velocity: "Black king, black jack, black heart;/We'd play it solitary while the dusks rushed by,/More than one-flesh-and-blood,/Almost one I." This poem, "Sister," contains already the mature Taylor *in nuce.* Here is the restless pentameter, skirting the iambic: "The path washed out, grown up, but not erased:/The wars of marriage and the family burst around us." Pentameter modulates to vernacular ditty ("When I was young, folks thought me pretty./I took my charms up to the city. . . . "), and then to tetrameter, trimeter, dimeter variations. Here, familiar to readers of her later poems, is the Southern world of enclosure in family, farm, and garden, and at the heart of it all, the explosive female voice, accepting and protesting: "I would have disfestooned my world." The poem's pace enacts, brilliantly, its conflicting forces: heart-thudding spondees ("Black king, black jack, black heart") resolve to a run of unstressed syllables and loose anapests ("We'd play it solitary while the . . . "), which give way in their turn to emphatic triple beats: "dusks rushed by," "Almost one I." In its counterpointing of speed and ritardando, "Sister" measures the pulse of consciousness, the mind that malingers and the mind that knows we rush onward toward extinction.

Taylor's poetry abounds in knowledge of such onrushing. Nor does it find it, necessarily, cause for mourning. "A Permanent Dye," from *Days Going / Days Coming Back* (1991), plays the pentameter of stability ("Just when I was thinking of immortality," "Don't be concerned. The dye is permanent.") against the nervous, fugitive free verse of mortality accepted:

> The running berries of the ditches,
> the hurrying weedbloom of her summer,
> moth-mullein and goat's rue,
> moths, fly-by-nights.

"A Permanent Dye," in its *double-entendres* ("rue," "fly-by-nights," "dye"), its cascading tercets, its participial speed, its delighted specificities, sings a hymn to transience, gives— paradoxically—a shape to transience, and celebrates our going as much as our staying. So does many an ode by Horace; but Taylor has turned urbane Horatian nonchalance into a feminine vernacular, intimate, homely, grounded in love: "The newborn scarf falls from the tissue:/'Like the one, you know, Grandmother had.'"

For all their shapeliness, Taylor's poems twist the language hard, until it lets loose the yelp of the true. Quick as a wink, she'll turn an adverb into an almost-noun ("My youth and the dead thereof,/the farflung thereof," from "How Morning Comes, Out of Sleep"). Nouns are likely to erupt into verbs ("A hound ears-up and/passions after," from "The Ghost"). At times, her parts of speech seem to be playing all parts at once; in the concluding lines of "Going, Dark," each major word seems to be doing multiple duty as adjective, noun, *and* verb, all at once:

> Dark
> in its cell of stars
> wheels,
> a falling of blocks:
> dulls of negligence,
> dooms of release,
> dooms of pardon,
> tombs of indifference.

Along with such syntactic mobility, Taylor compounds her images into an almost Anglo-Saxon density. Corn is "piled, foreskinned, altar high" in "Harvest, 1925"; as for flowers, "And the peony's the same blood-hoard,/tight-fisted, not to waste/its poor dirt budget," in "Flowers to Your Grave." For all their sociability, these poems spell danger, wildness, sacrificial fire; they see the world in a blaze; they deal in elementals. Her new book, *Late Leisure*, is anything but leisurely. It has its mortal fire as well as its blank spaces: "You take your cache that flares and flashes/out   a recent breath" ("These Gifts"). But never does its intensity overwhelm its generosity or its wit. Who but Taylor, in a book brimming with bereavement, would see a foam hot dog carton as a casket skipping down the sidewalk in wind; who but Taylor's persona, in this same casket poem, would observe a young man walking with a twisted shoulder, a bitter mouth, and admonish her subject: "Don't shiver little star/It's not as cold as all that."

To quote these lines from "Diary Entry, March 24" in a surround of prose, is to distort them by punctuating. On their own, they float mysteriously free from such directive, extending beyond the page, beyond the immediate subject. If we want poems written in the light of life and in the equal radiance cast by death, poems that cut beyond the literary to bring us news of survival, poems hip to the world's sorrow as to its plenitude and oddness, Taylor's should fill the bill. It is not a bill easily filled these days. We owe all the more gratitude, I think, to Eleanor Ross Taylor.

Between Two Worlds: The Poetry of Eleanor Ross Taylor

For a devoted minority of readers, the preeminent woman poet in the senior generation might be—not any of the predictable choices, but a reticent Southerner, who prefers needlework and gardening to the reading circuit, and who has lived for more than forty years with her husband in such university towns as Charlottesville, Greensboro, Sewanee, and Gainesville. Eleanor Taylor's poetry has been notoriously hard to come by. Her first volume, lavishly praised by Randall Jarrell, was unavailable because of copyright difficulties for many years. Her *New and Selected Poems* (1983) came out with the small Southern publisher Stuart Wright, and was reviewed in almost no major periodicals. Now the University of Utah Press Poetry Series has remedied all that, bringing together eighty-some pages of new work, plus a generous selection from all three previous volumes.

After such praise, it may be best to begin with a poem. Here is "New Girls," from the 1983 volume:

> Devious, devious are
> primroses in shade
> collecting sunshine
> without sunshine.
> Sprawling on the grass
> they grip their books.
> The strings of summer
> ring without answer.
> Hello Juliana?
> Hello Augusta?
> What are you doing tomorrow?
> Sleeping,
>   sleeping.
>
> Numerous the shades
> under primroses,
> shifting sands and

> sets and seasons,
> reaching for the
> fellow pillow,
> reaching for the
> strings of summer,
> too treble, too shining
> for inside eyes.

Yet this poem, like many of Taylor's, is so utterly itself that I almost despair of persuading anyone to like it, who doesn't like it instantly. I suppose I could begin with the comparisons. The shade-loving plants, "collecting sunshine/without sunshine," and the mysterious sexual plenitude of the girls who spend the whole summer day "Sleeping,/sleeping." The "strings" the plants hook onto to grow, and the girls' telephone cords. The pathos and child-sensuality of the "fellow pillow." The wonderful *names*. Then I might point to the music. It was Randall Jarrell who first compared Eleanor Taylor's poetry to Thomas Hardy's, and the comparison fits these short lines, irregular at first, gathering to a sing-songy trochaic dimeter at the very point where the leaps of association become strangest ("shifting sands and/ sets and seasons"). Finally this music becomes the music of the girls' lives, and invokes itself, defying the reader to condescend: "too treble, too shining/for inside eyes." If this poem was modeled on John Crowe Ransom's exquisite, outmoded lyric "Blue Girls," it is a much tenderer, because more empathetic, elegy for what youth doesn't have—and for what it does.

The Hardy comparison is, of course, apt to much else as well. One thinks of his "wistlessness" and "norward," encountering the inimitable oddities that sparkle, like mica, through Taylor's lines and titles. The cross "ethered up" above the altar. "[S]he mollusks somewhere." "In the Echoes, Wintering." Like Hardy, she cherishes a rural, dialect culture, all the more tenderly the more powerless it seems in the face of urban cosmopolitanism; yet, like him, she never forgets the distortions it wreaked on individual yearnings for freedom, when it had power. Like him, too, she can never quite let go of Christianity, or of the dread of the void after death, the ghostliness cast back over life, that comes with the fading of literal belief. There is even a trace of his troubled erotic naturalism in "Harvest, 1925," a period piece about a farm woman taken in adultery,

> weeping, behind the plums,
> a lactate field mouse,
> shucks cleaving
> to her teats.

Both are poets caught "between two worlds," in Matthew Arnold's phrase, never quite able to prefer the modern, secular, permissive one, yet sharing its perspectives.

Eleanor Taylor once wrote a rather notorious bad review of Sylvia Plath's *Ariel*. (She did make a prescient exception for some of the quieter poems, "Elm," "A Birthday Present," "Totem.") Reading some of her own early poems like "Goodbye Family," it's easy to feel that Plath's brand of suicidal individualism, the "White Godiva" unpeeling all the claims of others, "Dead hands, dead stringencies," was for her a road not taken:

> The years to climb! The walls to catch at!
>   To cut free
> And drop through the cloak closet and cellar
>   Is better—
> Under the foundations of God's world
>   Lilily
> Swimming on my side, with ear on shoulder,
>   Eyes unlettered,
> And intellectuality an asterisk
>   Now blurred—
> It's no use God's whistling, "Come back, Fido,
>   "Come back,
> "I won't tease any more." I'm in the glade
>   Remembering
> I meant to tell my daughter, "I looked for
>   You a cattail
> But they were all silked out" —
>   And now the water
> Meeting me around the curve, roaring, blanks
>   Out all but ear:
>   Not in the day time, not in the dark time
>   Will my voice cut and my poison puff
>   My treasures of flesh
>   My gems of flashing translucent spirit,
>   Nor my caress shatter them.

That primal unity, "under the foundations," where such musical tautologies as "Lilily" can happen; that lyric, suicidal escape, fueled as much by self-hatred, hatred of the "poison" hidden even in the frustrated ego's brilliance and kindness, as by resentment of others—all that would, some years later, be Plath's temptation, the "cauldron of morning" in which the "I" and everything else is melted down at the end of "Ariel."

For Eleanor Taylor, it is a rare mood, after *Wilderness of Ladies*. In her transitional volume, *Welcome Eumenides*, some poems even fly to the opposite extreme of unambivalent moral conservatism ("The Young Writer's Reply"). But in the poems of her prolific late flowering, from about 1974 on, her vision remains double, examining with anger and fierce empathy the spiritual lives of those who do not flee their backgrounds, or the constraints of family and class. Consider "When Robins Return," an elegy for an "eccentric," mother-dominated bachelor who wished to be reincarnated as a bird:

> I wonder when I hear at dawn in May
> that volubility at serious play
> whether it's born verbal charm to tempt
> earthworms, his Methodist constraint to pray. . . .
> . . . . .
> I see him flying with his lady mother
> south, falls, to the Gulf. They doff their feathers
> (at last she thinks him lyrical and bold)
> evenings under magnolia weather,
>
> play two-hand bridge, shuffling the red and black
> cards with goldish talons. The fatal pack
> is marked a different way this go-around:
> justly, he'll eat her while she's fighting back.

How delicately this poem appreciates the man, while telling all of the terrible unspoken truths about his life! How delicately, too, it handles all of the familiar tropes—nature as freedom, as what might absolve, in "serious play," the constrictions, the half-aggressions, half-deceptions of our socially warped selves; and against that the wish that that exact self could be held on to, could even get its own "back," for life's humiliations . . . It seems to me another near-perfect lyric, extending but deepening the line of Hardy and Ransom.

Taylor's characters are often victims, but her loyalties are too stubborn, too complex, for them ever to be the predictable, "politically correct" ones. Perhaps that is why two of her most ambitious poems, "Rachel Plummer's Dream" and "War Paint and Camouflage," seem to draw on those supremely unfashionable texts in which white settlers are the victims of Native Americans, not the other way around.

Rachel Plummer seems an almost inhuman extension of the "ladylike" virtues of avoiding self-pity, taking an interest in the world, until they become artist-virtues, mystic virtues. "You never shut your eyes./You always looked"—even when her husband and baby are brutally slaughtered. And she goes on noting it all down, in her copybook prose, "the Purest Are you ever breathed," "the Fine Springs, the Snow Rabbitt." She insists on being admitted to the Indian culture ("a dog that *would*"), though she draws certain lines: "refused the serving of roast enemy; it was a foot." (This is no *Dances with Wolves*, where the real atrocities are always committed by some other tribe.) And it is, finally, her need to "see" that makes her rebel violently, as she has not, of course, at any of her real torments. When her young Indian "mistress" is afraid to explore a mountain cave with her, Rachel beats the woman, then leads her "the miles back to the mouth," and then, alone,

> at last made your long way in that unearthly
> twinkling dark, beside the crystal river,
> to sound of mighty falls ahead,
> plunging
> how far?   into what unknown place?
> caught echoes of your dying baby's cries;
> like tranced Ezekiel in Babylon
> descried the noise of wings, of wings let down—
> *though briers and thorns be with thee, not afraid!*

What we know—though Rachel perhaps does not—is that "this parapsychologic episode" appropriates the form of a young Indian male's vision-quest. Yet the content of her self-healing is Christian, and, what is more, patriarchal. For all the powerfully feminist implications of inner space, caves, the waterfall vanishing into uncharted depth, it is a "He," a divine father/lover, who at last comes "to bathe/your wounds that never pained again." (In her own, first-person, attempt to "analyze," Taylor writes "I discount sex," making one at once love her brashness—not unlike Plummer's own—and feel she has missed the whole point of psychoanalytic thinking, if she thinks "sex" is separable from such other fundamental needs as nurturance and recognition.) In the end, Taylor seems to opt for Plummer's own, literally Christian explanation—

> that Resurrection flaring in the cave,
> those stars in earth, time stopped
> and you with eyes to see.

I think it is because Rachel Plummer's triumph fits no category that is entirely comfortable for the late twentieth-century reader, that it sticks so undislodgeably, at least in my mind. In her quiet way, Rachel is a challenge to all of those texts that would see nothing but a humiliating "identification with the oppressor" in the perversely complex loyalties women have shown, over the centuries. Beyond even gendered considerations, she becomes a kind of savage parable of the spirit, creating itself out of irreconcilable contradiction, out of what compromises, tortures, or violates it, because that is what it means to exist in space and time.

In the more recent poem, "War Paint and Camouflage" (when it first appeared in *The New Yorker*, it was called, more simply and movingly, "Captive Voices"), no such heroic transcendence seems possible. For these captives, "Mountains were never sublime and/forests did not breathe grandeur," because

> Raising the eyes and looking far
> requires a certain off-guard.
> Requires if not pleasure in, some
> concord with one's status quo.

The voices of real captivity, real torture, are juxtaposed, in "The Waste Land" manner, with contemporary voices. The risk is that the latter will simply be annihilated by the comparison. (One of them actually says, "People *suffered*," speaking of a five-day power outage.) Yet many of these voices are so inventive, so gifted with words—

> Well, the doctor didn't want me to become addicted.
> So it was Tantalus all over again, with the Tylenol

or

> You see two people were needed:
> somebody to take Dad to the hospital
> and somebody to stay with Mom.
> That's why it happened—
> I couldn't be two people

—that in the end they force our compassion, force us to acknowledge the common human denominators—pain, the fear of death, the desire to have enough under control for "a certain offguard." Even this paper world approaching the millennium, where "The hunger of the first part/sues the hunger of the second part," is as it is because "hunger," in all its senses, is fundamental and increasing. The poem ends with what can either be another abrupt voice, with an unexpectedly sharp cut at the prolifers (yes, you never are quite sure of the politics here), or, in dead earnest, the author's "prayer":

> I carry my prayer on a stick:
> Over-population is murder.

Given her empathy for trapped lives, given, also, her perennially divided perspective on historical change, it is small wonder that Taylor is one of the great contemporary elegists. Besides "When Robins Return," and the cryptic but heartbreaking elegy for Jarrell, "New Dust," I would recommend the family elegies, especially "Dry Nights," "Rack and Ruin," and "Limits." And then, in the odder genre of self-elegy—poems that try to come to terms with the poet's own blank future—"Pain in the House" and "Next Year," which ends a catalog of seemingly optimistic predictions with

I won't miss the ducks' migration:
stepping into the night by my gate I'll hear
  the appointed skytramping,
the comradely call; who knows?
it may be my year to share
  the vacant eye full of destination.

One could go on quoting forever; nearly every poem has at least one or two such stunning effects as "skytramping," or that "vacant"/"full" last line. But let me conclude, instead, with a mild complaint, at the omission of the longest and best of the family elegies from the Stuart Wright volume, "The Ribbon to Norwood." Reliving a long, slow bus trip to visit the poet's dying mother, the poem somehow subsumes the whole story of Southern womanhood, back to the stockade at Jamestown, that has been the burden of so much of Taylor's work. At a climactic point, the poem shifts to dialect, the quintessential mother tongue:

Goin Yanceyville
Don think my mama goin live very long.
  In her voice, some-old-lonesome
  freight train whooping at the crossing.
Will this loosestrife live?
  Now hit's a wild thing,
  a wild thing used to do-without.
To make them live. To hold them back.
They pull me on.

"Hit," here, appears to be the dying mother's spirit; but it could equally well be the suicidal wife of "Goodbye Family," or the anonymous maker of "The Altar Needlework," or Rachel Plummer, or the poet herself. "Hit" is the new note, proud and solitary, yet in its very elusiveness somehow reconciling the claims of detachment and allegiance, that Eleanor Ross Taylor has added to the poetry of American women, and to American poetry per se.

CONTRIBUTORS

Betty Adcock is the author of five volumes of poetry from Louisiana State University Press, including *Intervale: New and Selected Poems*. She has taught in the Warren Wilson MFA Program for writers and is Kenan Writer in Residence at Meredith College in Raleigh, North Carolina. Her work has received the Texas Institute of Letters Prize and the North Carolina Award for Literature.

Fred Chappell is a native of North Carolina and has taught at the University of North Carolina-Greensboro for 36 years. He has published numerous volumes of poetry, fiction, and criticism. His latest novel is *Look Back All the Green Valley*, and his latest book of poetry, *Family Gathering*.

Ben Cleary is a writer and teacher who lives in Hanover County, Virginia. He got to know Peter and Eleanor Taylor while he was a graduate student in English at the University of Virginia in the late 1970s. His stories and commentaries have aired on National Public Radio, and his articles have appeared in periodicals as varied as *Civil War* and *Reggae Report*.

Alfredo Franco directs adult educational programs at The Virginia Museum of Fine Arts in Richmond, Virginia. A collection of his poetry was published by the Aulos Press in Mexico City.

Lorrie Goldensohn publishes poetry and criticism in a variety of journals. Her most recent book is a critical study entitled *Elizabeth Bishop: The Biography of a Poetry*. Two books are forthcoming: a collection of poems, *Occupying Forces*, and a study of twentieth-century war literature, *Dismantling Glory*.

Eric Gudas's poems, literary interviews, and reviews have appeared in *The American Poetry Review*, *Crazy Horse*, *The Iowa Review*, *Poetry Flash*, and elsewhere. He lives in Davis, California.

James Harms is the author of three books of poetry from Carnegie Mellon University Press, the latest of which is *Quarters*. He directs the creative writing program at West Virginia University.

Richard Howard, winner of the Pulitzer Prize, is the author of eleven books of poems, numerous translations and reviews, and a study of American poetry since World War II. He is poetry editor of *Western Humanities Review* and *The Paris Review* and was director of the Braziller Poetry Series when it published Taylor's volume *Welcome Eumenides* in 1972.

Randall Jarrell (1914-1965) received the National Book Award for his book of poems, *The Woman at the Washington Zoo*. The author of children's books, a novel, and critical prose as well, he remains, as Adrienne Rich has written, "the conscience of poetry."

Heather Ross Miller is the author of fifteen books of poetry and fiction, including most recently *Champeen* and *Crusoe's Island*. The holder of three NEA creative writing fellowships, Miller also received the North Carolina Award for Literature. She currently teaches at Washington and Lee University in Virginia.

Gregory Orr is the author of six collections of poetry, most recently *City of Salt*. He has also published two collections of critical prose, *Stanley Kunitz: An Introduction to the Poetry* and *Richer Entanglements: Essays and Notes on Poetry and Poems,* and is co-editor with Ellen Bryant Voigt of *Self and the World: Poets Teaching Poets*. He teaches at the University of Virginia and is poetry editor of the *Virginia Quarterly Review*.

Adrienne Rich's most recent books of poetry are *Midnight Salvage: Poems 1995-1998* and *Fox: Poems 1998-2000*. A new selection of her essays, *Arts of the Possible: Essays and Conversations,* was published in 2001. She has recently been the recipient of the Dorothea Tanning Prize and of the Lannan Foundation Lifetime Achievement Award. She lives in California.

Deborah Tall's fourth book of poems, *Summons*, was chosen for the Kathryn A. Morton Poetry Prize by Charles Simic and published by Sarabande Books. She is also author of *The Island of the White Cow: Memories of an Irish Island* and *From Where We Stand: Recovering a Sense of Place*. Tall is the editor of *Seneca Review* and co-editor of *The Poet's Notebook*.

Henry Taylor is professor of literature and co-director of the Graduate Program in Creative Writing at American University. His books of poems include *The Horse Show at Midnight, An Afternoon of Pocket Billiards, The Flying Change*, which won the Pulitzer Prize, *Understanding Fiction: Poems, 1986-1996*, and *Brief Candles: 101 Clerihews*. His translations are also widely published.

Jean Valentine has published nine volumes of poetry, most recently *The Cradle of Real Life*. She has won numerous awards for her work, including the Yale Younger Poets Award for her first book and the Poetry Society's Shelly Memorial Award. She lives in New York City and teaches at Sarah Lawrence College, the Graduate Writing Program at New York University, and the 92nd Street Y.

Ellen Bryant Voigt is the author of five volumes of poetry, most recently *Kyrie*, a National Book Critics Circle Award Finalist, as well as *The Flexible Lyric*, a collection of essays on craft. She teaches in the Warren Wilson College low-residency MFA Program for Writers and is currently the Vermont State Poet.

Rosanna Warren teaches comparative literature at Boston University. Her most recent book of poems is *Stained Glass*, and she has also published translations and critical essays. Winner of numerous awards for her poetry, she is a Chancellor of the Academy of American Poets.

Alan Williamson is professor of English at the University of California at Davis. He is the author of four books of poetry, most recently, *Love and the Soul* and *Res Publica*, as well as four books of criticism.